Sixth Workshop on Computational Models of Reference, Anaphora and Coreference (CRAC 2023)

Singapore
6 - 7 December 2023

ISBN: 978-1-7138-8598-6

Printed from e-media with permission by:

Curran Associates, Inc.
57 Morehouse Lane
Red Hook, NY 12571

CURRAN ASSOCIATES INC. proceedings.com

Some format issues inherent in the e-media version may also appear in this print version.

Printed with permission by Curran Associates, Inc. (2024)

Association for Computational Linguistics
209 N. Eighth Street
Stroudsburg, Pennsylvania 18360

Phone: 1-570-476-8006
Fax: 1-570-476-0860

acl@aclweb.org

Additional copies of this publication are available from:

Curran Associates, Inc.
57 Morehouse Lane
Red Hook, NY 12571 USA
Phone: 845-758-0400
Fax: 845-758-2633
Email: curran@proceedings.com
Web: www.proceedings.com

EMNLP 2023

Proceedings of The Sixth Workshop on Computational Models of Reference, Anaphora and Coreference (CRAC 2023)

CRAC 2023, an EMNLP 2023 Workshop
December 6–7, 2023
Singapore

Message from the Program Chairs

This is the sixth edition of the Workshop on Computational Models of Reference, Anaphora and Coreference (CRAC). CRAC was first held in New Orleans five years ago in conjunction with NAACL HLT 2018. But the workshop series dates back to its predecessor, the Coreference Resolution Beyond OntoNotes (CORBON) that started in 2016, and has arguably become the primary forum for coreference researchers to present their latest results since the demise of the Discourse Anaphora and Anaphor Resolution Colloquium series in 2011. While CORBON focused on under-investigated coreference phenomena, CRAC has a broader scope, covering all cases of computational modeling of reference, anaphora, and coreference.

CRAC 2023 continued to attract a large number of very high quality papers. Specifically, we received 15 submissions which were rigorously reviewed by three program committee members. Based on their recommendations, we accepted 10 papers. Two papers were withdrawn. This is the first time we are experimenting with the presentation of a *non-archived* work in progress. The idea is to allow authors to submit their work in progress for review. If it gets accepted, they can present the work at the workshop. However, it won't be included in the workshop proceedings. Thus, they can still submit a more complete version as original work to another venue. Overall, we were pleased with the large number of submissions as well as the quality of the accepted papers.

This is the second year of the CRAC shared task on *Multilingual Coreference Resolution*. This allows researchers who did not participate in the workshop to disseminate their work to a smaller and more focused audience which should promote interesting discussions.

We are grateful to the following people, without whom we could not have assembled an interesting program for the workshop. First, we are indebted to our program committee members. This year the reviewing load was on an average of three papers per reviewer. All of them did the incredible job of completing their reviews in a short reviewing period. This year we have two invited talks. We thank Bernd Bohnet and Milan Straka for accepting our invitation to be this year's invited speakers. We continue the tradition of having a panel on the Universal Anaphora (UA) effort–a unified, language-independent markup scheme that reflects common cross-linguistic understanding of reference-related phenomena. Motivated by Universal Dependencies, UA aims to facilitate referential analysis of the similarities and idiosyncrasies among typologically different languages, support comparative evaluation of anaphora resolution systems and enable comparative linguistic studies. Finally, we would like to thank the workshop participants for joining us in this event.

We hope you will enjoy it as much as we do!

— Sameer Pradhan, Maciej Ogrodniczuk, Anna Nedoluzhko,
Massimo Poesio, and Vincent Ng

Organizers

Organizing Committee:

Maciej Ogrodniczuk, Institute of Computer Science, Polish Academy of Sciences, Poland
Vincent Ng, University of Texas at Dallas, USA
Sameer Pradhan, University of Pennsylvania and cemantix.org, USA
Massimo Poesio, Queen Mary University of London, UK
Anna Nedoluzhko, Charles University in Prague, Czechia

Program Committee:

Rahul Aralikatte, Mila – Quebec Artificial Intelligence Institute, Canada
Antonio Branco, University of Lisbon, Portugal
Arie Cattan, Bar-Ilan University, Israel
Haixia Chai, Heidelberg University, Germany
Yulia Grishina, Amazon, USA
Christian Hardmeier, IT University of Copenhagen, Denmark
Lars Hellan, Norwegian University of Science and Technology, Norway
Veronique Hoste, Ghent University, Belgium
Yufang Hou, IBM Research, Ireland
Ruihong Huang, Texas A&M University, USA
Sobha Lalitha Devi, Anna University of Chennai, India
Ekaterina Lapshinova-Koltunski, University of Hildesheim, Germany
Sharid Loáiciga, University of Gothenburg, Sweden.
Costanza Navaretta, University of Copenhagen, Denmark
Anna Nedoluzhko, Charles University in Prague, Czechia
Michal Novák, Charles University in Prague, Czechia
Massimo Poesio, Queen Mary University of London, UK
Ian Porada, Mila – Quebec Artificial Intelligence Institute, Canada
Yaqin Yang, Brandeis University, USA
Yilun Zhu, Georgetown University, USA
Heike Zinsmeister, University of Hamburg, Germany

Invited Talk

Multilingual Coreference Resolution with Innovative seq2seq Models

Bernd Bohnet, Google, USA

Abstract

In this talk, we explore advancements in coreference resolution systems, focusing on our novel approach that leverages a text-to-text (seq2seq) paradigm of modern LLMs. We utilize multilingual T5 (mT5) as the foundational language model. Traditional coreference systems primarily employ search algorithms across possible spans. In contrast, our method jointly predicts mentions and links, achieving superior accuracy on the CoNLL-2012 datasets. Notably, our system recorded an 83.3 F1-score for English, surpassing previous research. Further evaluations on multilingual datasets, particularly Arabic and Chinese, yielded improvements over prior works, showcasing the multilingual transfer abilities of our model across many languages. Additionally, our experiments with the SemEval-2010 datasets in various settings—including zero-shot and low resource transfer—reveal significant performance improvements for other languages. We will discuss the capabilities of LLMs to provide a more streamlined, effective, and unified approach to coreference resolution.

Speaker Bio

Bernd Bohnet is a researcher in Natural Language Processing (NLP). He earned his Ph.D. with a specialization in text generation. Subsequently, he served as an tenured Assistant Professor at the University of Birmingham. For the past nine years, Dr. Bohnet carried out research with Google and Google DeepMind. His expertise encompasses a broad range of topics in natural language understanding, including tagging, parsing, coreference resolution, and reading comprehension. In recent years, he has turned his attention to Large Language Models (LLMs), focusing on their capabilities in factual accuracy, question answering, and the integration techniques into LLMs (tool use).

Table of Contents

Workshop Program

Wednesday, Decmber 6, 2023

Opening Remarks

09:00–09:15 *Opening and Welcome*
Vincent Ng, Maciej Ogrodniczuk and Sameer Pradhan

Invited Talk

09:15–10:30 *Multilingual Coreference Resolution with Innovative seq2seq Models*
Bernd Bohnet

Short Break

10:30–11:00 *Coffee Break*

Paper Session I

11:00–11:10 *Filling in the Gaps: Efficient Event Coreference Resolution using Graph Autoencoder Networks*
Loic De Langhe, Orphee De Clercq and Veronique Hoste

11:10–11:20 *CAW-coref: Conjunction-Aware Word-level Coreference Resolution*
Karel D'Oosterlinck, Semere Kiros Bitew, Brandon Papineau, Christopher Potts, Thomas Demeester and Chris Develder

11:20–11:40 *Towards Transparency in Coreference Resolution: A Quantum-Inspired Approach*
Hadi Wazni and Mehrnoosh Sadrzadeh

11:40–12:00 *Scalar Anaphora: Annotating Degrees of Coreference in Text*
Bingyang Ye, Jingxuan Tu and James Pustejovsky

12:00–12:20 *Investigating Failures to Generalize for Coreference Resolution Models*
Ian Porada, Alexandra Olteanu, Kaheer Suleman, Adam Trischler and Jackie Chi Kit Cheung

Wednesday, Decmber 6, 2023 (continued)

12:20–12:30 *Better Handling Coreference Resolution in Aspect Level Sentiment Classification by Fine-Tuning Language Models*
Dhruv Mullick, Bilal Ghanem and Alona Fyshe

12:30–12:40 *The pragmatics of characters' mental perspectives in pronominal reference resolution*
Tiana Simovic and Craig Chambers

Long Break

12:40–14:00 *Lunch Break*

Paper Session II

14:00–14:10 *MARRS: Multimodal Reference Resolution System*
Halim Cagri Ates, Shruti Bhargava, Site Li, Jiarui Lu, Siddhardha Maddula, Joel Ruben Antony Moniz, Anil Kumar Nalamalapu, Roman Hoang Nguyen, Melis Ozyildirim, Alkesh Patel, Dhivya Piraviperumal, Vincent Renkens, Ankit Samal, Thy Tran, Bo-Hsiang Tseng, Hong Yu, Yuan Zhang and Shirley Zou

14:10–14:30 *Towards Harmful Erotic Content Detection through Coreference-Driven Contextual Analysis*
Inez Okulska and Emilia Wisnios

14:30–14:40 *Integrated Annotation of Event Structure, Object States, and Entity Coreference*
Kyeongmin Rim and James Pustejovsky

Findings Paper Session

14:40–14:50 *The Coreference under Transformation Labeling Dataset: Entity Tracking in Procedural Texts Using Event Models*
Kyeongmin Rim, Jingxuan Tu, Bingyang Ye, Marc Verhagen, Eben Holderness and James Pustejovsky

14:50–15:00 *ezCoref: Towards Unifying Annotation Guidelines for Coreference Resolution*
Ankita Gupta, Marzena Karpinska, Wenlong Zhao, Kalpesh Krishna, Jack Merullo, Luke Yeh, Mohit Iyyer and Brendan O'Connor

15:00–15:10 *Longtonotes: OntoNotes with Longer Coreference Chains*
Kumar Shridhar, Nicholas Monath, Raghuveer Thirukovalluru, Alessandro Stolfo, Manzil Zaheer, Andrew McCallum and Mrinmaya Sachan

15:10–15:20 *A Memory Model for Question Answering from Streaming Data Supported by Rehearsal and Anticipation of Coreference Information*
Vladimir Araujo, Alvaro Soto and Marie-Francine bMoens

15:20–15:30 *Investigating Multilingual Coreference Resolution by Universal Annotations*
Haixia Chai and Michael Strube

Short Break

15:30–16:00 *Coffee break*

Panel on Universal Anaphora

16:00–17:00 *Panel discussion*
moderated by Sameer Pradhan

Thursday, December 7, 2023

CRAC 2023 Shared Task on Multilingual Coreference Resolution

Invited talk

09:00–09:30 *Recent Computational Approaches to Coreference Resolution*
Milan Straka

Overview Paper Talk

09:30–10:30 *Findings of the Second Shared Task on Multilingual Coreference Resolution*
Zdeněk Žabokrtský, Miloslav Konopík, Anna Nedoluzhko, Michal Novák, Maciej Ogrodniczuk, Martin Popel, Ondřej Pražák, Jakub Sido, Daniel Zeman and Yilun Zhu

Short Break

10:30–11:00 *Coffee Break*

Shared Task System Demonstration Session

11:00–11:20 *Multilingual coreference resolution: Adapt and Generate*
Natalia Skachkova, Tatiana Anikina and Anna Mokhova

11:20–11:40 *Neural End-to-End Coreference Resolution using Morphological Information*
Tuğba Pamay Arslan, Kutay Acar and Gülşen Eryiğit

11:40–12:00 *ÚFAL CorPipe at CRAC 2023: Larger Context Improves Multilingual Coreference Resolution*
Milan Straka

12:00–12:20 *McGill at CRAC 2023: Multilingual Generalization of Entity-Ranking Coreference Resolution Models*
Ian Porada and Jackie Chi Kit Cheung

Closing Remarks

12:20–12:30 *Closing the workshop*
Maciej Ogrodniczuk, Sameer Pradhan and Vincent Ng

Filling in the Gaps:
Efficient Event Coreference Resolution using Graph Autoencoder Networks

Loic De Langhe, Orphée De Clercq, Veronique Hoste
LT3, Language and Translation Technology Team, Ghent University, Belgium
Groot-Brittanniëlaan 45, 9000 Ghent, Belgium
firstname.lastname@ugent.be

Abstract

We introduce a novel and efficient method for Event Coreference Resolution (ECR) applied to a lower-resourced language domain. By framing ECR as a graph reconstruction task, we are able to combine deep semantic embeddings with structural coreference chain knowledge to create a parameter-efficient family of Graph Autoencoder models (GAE). Our method significantly outperforms classical mention-pair methods on a large Dutch event coreference corpus in terms of overall score, efficiency and training speed. Additionally, we show that our models are consistently able to classify more difficult coreference links and are far more robust in low-data settings when compared to transformer-based mention-pair coreference algorithms.

1 Introduction

Event coreference resolution (ECR) is a discourse-centered NLP task in which the goal is to determine whether or not two textual events refer to the same real-life or fictional event. While this is a fairly easy task for human readers, it is far more complicated for AI algorithms, which often do not have access to the extra-linguistic knowledge or discourse structure overview that is required to successfully connect these events. Nonetheless ECR, especially when considering cross-documents settings, holds interesting potential for a large variety of practical NLP applications such as summarization (Liu and Lapata, 2019), information extraction (Humphreys et al., 1997) and content-based news recommendation (Vermeulen, 2018).

However, despite the many potential avenues for ECR, the task remains highly understudied for comparatively lower-resourced languages. Furthermore, in spite of significant strides made since the advent of transformer-based coreference systems, a growing number of studies has questioned the effectiveness of such models. It has been suggested that classification decisions are still primarily based on the surface-level lexical similarity between the textual spans of event mentions (Ahmed et al., 2023; De Langhe et al., 2023), while this is far from the only aspect that should be considered in the classification decision. Concretely, in many models coreferential links are assigned between similar mentions even when they are not coreferent, leading to a significant number of false positive classifications, such as between Examples 1 and 2.

1. The French president Macron met with the American president for the first time today

2. French President Sarkozy met the American president

We believe that the fundamental problem with this method stems from the fact that in most cases events are only compared in a pairwise manner and not as part of a larger coreference chain. The evidence that transformer-based coreference resolution is primarily based on superficial similarity leads us to believe that the current pairwise classification paradigm for transformer-based event coreference is highly inefficient, especially for studies in lower-resourced languages where the state of the art still often relies on the costly process of fine-tuning large monolingual BERT-like models (De Langhe et al., 2022b).

In this paper we aim to both address the lack of studies in comparatively lower-resourced languages, as well as the more fundamental concerns w.r.t. the task outlined above. We frame ECR as a graph reconstruction task and introduce a family of graph autoencoder models which consistently outperforms the traditional transformer-based methods on a large Dutch ECR corpus, both in terms of accuracy and efficiency. Additionally, we introduce a language-agnostic model variant which disregards the use of semantic features entirely and even outperforms transformer-based classification in some

Proceedings of the Sixth Workshop on Computational Models of Reference, Anaphora and Coreference (CRAC 2023), pages 1–7
December 6–7, 2023

situations. Quantitative analysis reveals that the lightweight autoencoder models can consistently classify more difficult mentions (cfr. Examples 1 and 2) and are far more robust in low-data settings compared to traditional mention-pair algorithms.

2 Related Work

2.1 Event Coreference Resolution

The primary paradigm for event coreference resolution takes the form of a binary mention-pair approach. This method generates all possible event pairs and reduces the classification to a binary decision (coreferent or not) between each event pair. A large variety of classical machine learning algorithms has been tested using the mention-pair paradigm such as decision trees (Cybulska and Vossen, 2015), support vector machines (Chen et al., 2015) and standard deep neural networks (Nguyen et al., 2016).

More recent work has focused on the use of LLMs and transformer encoders (Cattan et al., 2021a,b), with span-based architectures attaining the best overall results (Joshi et al., 2020; Lu and Ng, 2021). It has to be noted that mention-pair approaches relying on LLMs suffer most from the limitations discussed in Section 1. In an effort to mitigate these issues some studies have sought to move away from the pairwise computation of coreference by modelling coreference chains as graphs instead. These methods' primary goal is to create a structurally-informed representation of the coreference chains by integrating the overall document (Fan et al., 2022; Tran et al., 2021) or discourse (Huang et al., 2022) structure. Other graph-based methods have focused on commonsense reasoning (Wu et al., 2022).

Research for comparatively lower-resourced languages has generally followed the paradigms and methods described above and has focused on languages such as Chinese (Mitamura et al., 2015), Arabic (NIST, 2005) and Dutch (Minard et al., 2016).

2.2 Graph Autoencoders

Graph Autoencoder models were introduced by Kipf and Welling (2016b) as an efficient method for graph reconstruction tasks. The original paper introduces both variational graph autoencoders (VGAE) and non-probabilistic graph autoencoders (GAE) networks. The models are parameterized by a 2-layer graph-convolutional network (GCN) (Kipf and Welling, 2016a) encoder and a generative inner-product decoder between the latent variables. While initially conceived as lightweight models for citation network prediction tasks, both the VGAE and GAE have been successfully applied to a wide variety of applications such as molecule design (Liu et al., 2018), social network relational learning (Yang et al., 2020) and 3D scene generation (Chattopadhyay et al., 2023). Despite their apparent potential for effectively processing large amounts of graph-structured data, application within the field of NLP has been limited to a number of studies in unsupervised relational learning (Li et al., 2020).

3 Experiments

3.1 Data

Our data consists of the Dutch ENCORE corpus (De Langhe et al., 2022a), which in its totality consists of 12,875 annotated events spread over 1,015 documents that were sourced from a collection of Dutch (Flemish) newspaper articles. Coreferential relations between events were annotated at the within-document and cross-document level.

3.2 Experimental Setup

3.2.1 Baseline Coreference Model

Our baseline model consists of the Dutch monolingual BERTje model (de Vries et al., 2019) finetuned for cross-document ECR. First, each possible event pair in the data is encoded by concatenating the two events and by subsequently feeding these to the BERTje encoder. We use the token representation of the classification token *[CLS]* as the aggregate embedding of each event pair, which is subsequently passed to a softmax-activated classification function. Finally, the results of the text pair classification are passed through a standard agglomerative clustering algorithm (Kenyon-Dean et al., 2018; Barhom et al., 2019) in order to obtain output in the form of coreference chains.

We also train two parameter-efficient versions of this baseline model using the distilled Dutch Language model RobBERTje (Delobelle et al., 2022) and a standard BERTje model trained with bottleneck adapters (Pfeiffer et al., 2020).

3.2.2 Graph Autoencoder Model

We make the assumption that a coreference chain can be represented by an undirected, unweighted graph $\mathcal{G} = (V, E)$ with $|V|$ nodes, where each node represents an event and each edge $e \in E$ between

Model	CONLL F1	Training Runtime (s)	Inference Runtime (s)	Trainable Parameters	Disk Space (MB)
MP RobBERTje	0.767	7962	16.31	74M	297
MP BERTje$_{ADPT}$	0.780	12 206	20.61	0.9M	3.5
MP BERTje	0.799	9737	21.78	110M	426
GAE NoFeatures	0.832 ± 0.008	1006	0.134	825856	3.2
GAE BERTje$_{768}$	0.835 ± 0.010	975	0.263	51200	0.204
GAE BERTje$_{3072}$	**0.852 ± 0.006**	1055	0.294	198656	0.780
GAE RobBERT$_{768}$	0.838 ± 0.004	1006	0.273	51200	0.204
GAE RobBERT$_{3072}$	0.841 ± 0.007	1204	0.292	198656	0.780
GAE SBERT	0.801 ± 0.002	982	0.291	51200	0.204
VGAE NoFeatures	0.824 ± 0.009	1053	0.139	827904	3.2
VGAE BERTje$_{768}$	0.822 ± 0.011	1233	0.282	53248	0.212
VGAE BERTje$_{3072}$	0.842 ± 0.009	1146	0.324	200704	0.788
VGAE RobBERT$_{768}$	0.828 ± 0.0021	1141	0.288	53248	0.212
VGAE RobBERT$_{3072}$	0.831 ± 0.004	1209	0.301	200704	0.788
VGAE SBERT	0.773 ± 0.012	1185	0.295	53248	0.212

Table 1: Results for the cross-document event coreference task. We report the average CONLL score and standard deviation over 3 training runs with different random seed initialization for the GCN weight matrices (GAE/VAE) and classification heads (Mention-Pair models). Inference runtime is reported for the entire test set.

two nodes denotes a coreferential link between those events. We frame ECR as a graph reconstruction task where a partially masked adjacency matrix A and a node-feature matrix X are used to predict all original edges in the graph. We employ both the VGAE and GAE models discussed in Section 2.2. In a non-probabilistic setting (GAE) the coreference graph is obtained by passing the adjacency matrix A and node-feature matrix X through a Graph Convolutional Neural Network (GCN) encoder and then computing the reconstructed matrix $\hat{A}$ from the latent embeddings Z:

$$Z = GCN(X, A) \quad (1)$$

$$\hat{A} = \sigma(ZZ^T) \quad (2)$$

For a detailed overview of the (probabilistic) variational graph autoencoder we refer the reader to the original paper by Kipf and Welling (2016b).

Our experiments are performed in a cross-document setting, meaning that the input adjacency matrix A contains all events in the ENCORE dataset. Following the original approach by Kipf and Welling (2016b) we mask 15% of the edges, 5% to be used for validation and the remaining 10% for testing. An equal amount of non-edges is randomly sampled from A to balance the validation and test data.

We extract masked edges and non-edges and use them to build the training, validation and test sets for the mention-pair baseline models detailed above, ensuring that both the mention-pair and graph autoencoder models have access to exactly the same data for training, validation and testing. We define the encoder network with a 64-dimension hidden layer and 32-dimension latent variables. For all experiments we train for a total duration of 200 epochs using an Adam optimizer (Kingma and Ba, 2014) and a learning rate of 0.001.

We construct node features through Dutch monolingual transformer models by average-pooling token representations for each token in the event span in the models' final hidden layer, resulting in a 768-dimensional feature vector for each node in the graph. For this we use the Dutch BERTje model (de Vries et al., 2019), a Dutch sentence-BERT model (Reimers and Gurevych, 2019) and the Dutch RoBERTa-based RobBERT model (Delobelle et al., 2020). Additionally, we create a second feature set for the BERTje and RobBERT models where each event is represented by the concatenation of the last 4 layers' average-pooled token representations Devlin et al. (2018). This in turn results in a 3072-dimensional feature vector.

Finally, we also evaluate a language-agnostic featureless model where X is represented by the identity matrix of A.

3.2.3 Hardware Specifications

The baseline coreference algorithms were trained and evaluated on 2 Tesla V100-SXM2-16GB GPUs. Due to GPU memory constraints, the Graph encoder models were all trained and evaluated on a single 2.6 GHz 6-Core Intel Core i7 CPU.

4 Results and Discussion

Results from our experiments are disclosed in Table 1. Results are reported through the CONLL F1 metric, an average of 3 commonly used metrics for coreference evaluation: MUC (Vilain et al., 1995),

B^3 (Bagga and Baldwin, 1998) and CEAF (Luo, 2005). We find that the graph autoencoder models consistently outperform the traditional mention-pair approach. Moreover, we find the autoencoder approach significantly reduces model size, training time and inference speed even when compared to parameter-efficient transformer-based methods. We note that the VGAE models perform slightly worse compared to their non-probabilistic counterparts, which is contrary to the findings in Kipf and Welling (2016b). This can be explained by the use of more complex acyclic graph data in the original paper. In this more uncertain context, probabilistic models would likely perform better.

As a means of quantitative error analysis, we report the average Levenshtein distance between two event spans for the True Positive (TP) pairs in our test set in Figure 1. Logically, if graph-based models are able to better classify harder (i.e non-similar) edges, the average Levenstein distance for predicted TP edges should be higher than for the mention-pair models. For readability's sake we only include results for the best performing GAE-class models. A more detailed table can be found in the Appendix. We find that the average distance between TP pairs increases for our introduced graph models, indicating that graph-based models can, to some extent, mitigate the pitfalls of mention-pair methodologies as discussed in Section 1.

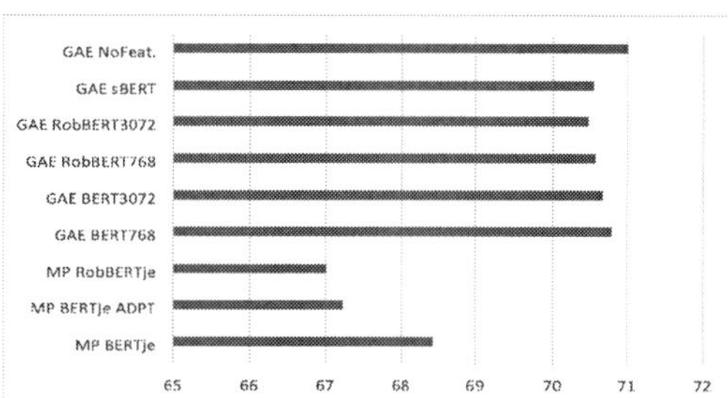

Figure 1: Average Levenshtein distance for True Positive (TP) classifications across all models

5 Ablation Studies

We gauge the robustness of the graph-based models in low-data settings by re-running the original experiment and continually reducing the available training data by increments of 10%. Figure 2 shows the CONLL F1 score for each of the models with respect to the available training data size. Also here, only the best-performing GAE-class models are visualized and an overview of all models' performance can be found in the Appendix. Surprisingly, we find that training the model on as little as 5% of the total amount of edges in the dataset can already lead to satisfactory results. Logically, feature-less models suffer from a significant drop in performance when available training data is reduced. We also find that the overall drop in performance is far greater for the traditional mention-pair model than it is for the feature-based GAE-class models in low-data settings. Overall, we conclude that the introduced family of models can be a lightweight and stable alternative to traditional mention-pair coreference models, even in settings with little to no available training data.

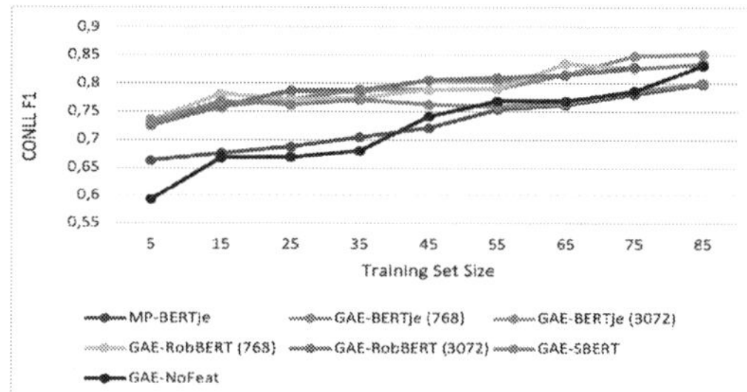

Figure 2: CONLL F1 performance with respect to the available training data.

6 Conclusion

We show that ECR through graph autoencoders significantly outperforms traditional mention-pair approaches in terms of performance, speed and model size in settings where coreference chains are at least partially known. Our method provides a fast and lightweight approach for processing large cross-document collections of event data. Additionally, our analysis shows that combining BERT-like embeddings and structural knowledge of coreference chains mitigates the issues in mention-pair classification w.r.t the dependence on surface-form lexical similarity. Our ablation experiments reveal that only a very small number of training edges is needed to obtain satisfactory performance.

Future work will explore the possibility of combining mention-pair models with the proposed graph autoencoder approach in a pipeline setting in order to make it possible to employ graph reconstruction models in settings where initially all edges in the graph are unknown. Additionally, we aim to perform more fine-grained analyses, both quantitative and qualitative, regarding the type of errors made by graph-based coreference models.

7 Limitations

We identify two possible limitations with the work presented above. First, by framing coreference resolution as a graph reconstruction task we assume that at least some coreference links in the cross-document graph are available to train on. However, we note that this issue can in part be mitigated by a simple exact match heuristic for event spans on unlabeled data. Moreover, in most application settings it is not inconceivable that at least a partial graph is available.

A second limitation stems from the fact that we modelled coreference chains as undirected graphs. It could be argued that some coreferential relationships such as pronominal anaphora could be more accurately modelled using directed graphs instead.

Acknowledgements

This work was supported by Ghent University under grant BOFGOA2018000601 and by the Research Foundation–Flanders under project grant number FWO.OPR.2020.0014.01.

References

Shafiuddin Rehan Ahmed, Abhijnan Nath, James H Martin, and Nikhil Krishnaswamy. 2023. $2 * n$ is better than nΘ2: Decomposing event coreference resolution into two tractable problems. *arXiv preprint arXiv:2305.05672*.

Amit Bagga and Breck Baldwin. 1998. Algorithms for scoring coreference chains. In *The first international conference on language resources and evaluation workshop on linguistics coreference*, volume 1, pages 563–566. Citeseer.

Shany Barhom, Vered Shwartz, Alon Eirew, Michael Bugert, Nils Reimers, and Ido Dagan. 2019. Revisiting joint modeling of cross-document entity and event coreference resolution. *arXiv preprint arXiv:1906.01753*.

Arie Cattan, Alon Eirew, Gabriel Stanovsky, Mandar Joshi, and Ido Dagan. 2021a. Cross-document coreference resolution over predicted mentions. *arXiv preprint arXiv:2106.01210*.

Arie Cattan, Alon Eirew, Gabriel Stanovsky, Mandar Joshi, and Ido Dagan. 2021b. Realistic evaluation principles for cross-document coreference resolution. *arXiv preprint arXiv:2106.04192*.

Aditya Chattopadhyay, Xi Zhang, David Paul Wipf, Himanshu Arora, and René Vidal. 2023. Learning graph variational autoencoders with constraints and structured priors for conditional indoor 3d scene generation. In *Proceedings of the IEEE/CVF Winter Conference on Applications of Computer Vision*, pages 785–794.

Yubo Chen, Liheng Xu, Kang Liu, Daojian Zeng, and Jun Zhao. 2015. Event Extraction via Dynamic Multi-Pooling Convolutional Neural Networks. *Proceedings of the 53rd Annual Meeting of the Association for Computational Linguistics and the 7th International Joint Conference on Natural Language Processing*, pages 167–176.

Agata Cybulska and Piek Vossen. 2015. Translating Granularity of Event Slots into Features for Event Coreference Resolution. In *Proceedings of the The 3rd Workshop on EVENTS: Definition, Detection, Coreference, and Representation*, pages 1–10, Denver, Colorado. Association for Computational Linguistics.

Loic De Langhe, Orphée De Clercq, and Veronique Hoste. 2022a. Constructing a cross-document event coreference corpus for dutch. *Language Resources and Evaluation*, pages 1–30.

Loic De Langhe, Orphée De Clercq, and Veronique Hoste. 2022b. Investigating cross-document event coreference for dutch.

Loic De Langhe, Thierry Desot, Orphée De Clercq, and Veronique Hoste. 2023. A benchmark for dutch end-to-end cross-document event coreference resolution. *Electronics*, 12(4).

Wietse de Vries, Andreas van Cranenburgh, Arianna Bisazza, Tommaso Caselli, Gertjan van Noord, and Malvina Nissim. 2019. Bertje: A dutch bert model. *arXiv preprint arXiv:1912.09582*.

Pieter Delobelle, Thomas Winters, and Bettina Berendt. 2020. Robbert: a dutch roberta-based language model. *arXiv preprint arXiv:2001.06286*.

Pieter Delobelle, Thomas Winters, and Bettina Berendt. 2022. Robbertje: A distilled dutch bert model. *arXiv preprint arXiv:2204.13511*.

Jacob Devlin, Ming-Wei Chang, Kenton Lee, and Kristina Toutanova. 2018. Bert: Pre-training of deep bidirectional transformers for language understanding. *arXiv preprint arXiv:1810.04805*.

Chuang Fan, Jiaming Li, Xuan Luo, and Ruifeng Xu. 2022. Enhancing structure preservation in coreference resolution by constrained graph encoding. *IEEE/ACM Transactions on Audio, Speech, and Language Processing*, 30:2557–2567.

Congcheng Huang, Sheng Xu, Longwang He, Peifeng Li, and Qiaoming Zhu. 2022. Incorporating generation method and discourse structure to event coreference resolution. In *International Conference on Neural Information Processing*, pages 73–84. Springer.

Kevin Humphreys, Robert Gaizauskas, and Saliha Azzam. 1997. Event coreference for information extraction. In *Proceedings of the ACL/EACL Workshop on Operational Factors in Practical, Robus Anaphora Resolution for Unrestricted Texts*, pages 75–81.

Mandar Joshi, Danqi Chen, Yinhan Liu, Daniel S Weld, Luke Zettlemoyer, and Omer Levy. 2020. Spanbert: Improving pre-training by representing and predicting spans. *Transactions of the Association for Computational Linguistics*, 8:64–77.

Kian Kenyon-Dean, Jackie Chi Kit Cheung, and Doina Precup. 2018. Resolving Event Coreference with Supervised Representation Learning and Clustering-Oriented Regularization. In *Proceedings of the Seventh Joint Conference on Lexical and Computational Semantics*, pages 1–10, New Orleans, Louisiana. Association for Computational Linguistics.

Diederik P Kingma and Jimmy Ba. 2014. Adam: A method for stochastic optimization. *arXiv preprint arXiv:1412.6980*.

Thomas N Kipf and Max Welling. 2016a. Semi-supervised classification with graph convolutional networks. *arXiv preprint arXiv:1609.02907*.

Thomas N Kipf and Max Welling. 2016b. Variational graph auto-encoders. *arXiv preprint arXiv:1611.07308*.

Irene Li, Alexander Fabbri, Swapnil Hingmire, and Dragomir Radev. 2020. R-vgae: Relational-variational graph autoencoder for unsupervised prerequisite chain learning. *arXiv preprint arXiv:2004.10610*.

Qi Liu, Miltiadis Allamanis, Marc Brockschmidt, and Alexander Gaunt. 2018. Constrained graph variational autoencoders for molecule design. *Advances in neural information processing systems*, 31.

Yang Liu and Mirella Lapata. 2019. Hierarchical transformers for multi-document summarization. *arXiv preprint arXiv:1905.13164*.

Jing Lu and Vincent Ng. 2021. Conundrums in event coreference resolution: Making sense of the state of the art. In *Proceedings of the 2021 Conference on Empirical Methods in Natural Language Processing*, pages 1368–1380.

Xiaoqiang Luo. 2005. On coreference resolution performance metrics. In *Proceedings of Human Language Technology Conference and Conference on Empirical Methods in Natural Language Processing*, pages 25–32.

Anne-Lyse Minard, Manuela Speranza, Ruben Urizar, Marieke van Erp, Anneleen Schoen, and Chantal van Son. 2016. MEANTIME, the NewsReader Multilingual Event and Time Corpus. In *Proceedings of the 10th language resources and evaluation conference (LREC 2016)*, page 6, Portorož, Slovenia. European Language Resources Association (ELRA).

Teruko Mitamura, Yukari Yamakawa, Susan Holm, Zhiyi Song, Ann Bies, Seth Kulick, and Stephanie Strassel. 2015. Event Nugget Annotation: Processes and Issues. In *Proceedings of the The 3rd Workshop on EVENTS: Definition, Detection, Coreference, and Representation*, pages 66–76, Denver, Colorado. Association for Computational Linguistics.

Thien Huu Nguyen, Adam Meyers, and Ralph Grishman. 2016. New york university 2016 system for kbp event nugget: A deep learning approach. In *TAC*.

NIST. 2005. The ACE 2005 (ACE 05) Evaluation Plan.

Jonas Pfeiffer, Andreas Rücklé, Clifton Poth, Aishwarya Kamath, Ivan Vulić, Sebastian Ruder, Kyunghyun Cho, and Iryna Gurevych. 2020. Adapterhub: A framework for adapting transformers. *arXiv preprint arXiv:2007.07779*.

Nils Reimers and Iryna Gurevych. 2019. Sentence-bert: Sentence embeddings using siamese bert-networks. *arXiv preprint arXiv:1908.10084*.

Hieu Minh Tran, Duy Phung, and Thien Huu Nguyen. 2021. Exploiting document structures and cluster consistencies for event coreference resolution. In *Proceedings of the 59th Annual Meeting of the Association for Computational Linguistics and the 11th International Joint Conference on Natural Language Processing (Volume 1: Long Papers)*, pages 4840–4850.

Judith Vermeulen. 2018. newsdna : promoting news diversity : an interdisciplinary investigation into algorithmic design, personalization and the public interest (2018-2022).

Marc Vilain, John D Burger, John Aberdeen, Dennis Connolly, and Lynette Hirschman. 1995. A model-theoretic coreference scoring scheme. In *Sixth Message Understanding Conference (MUC-6): Proceedings of a Conference Held in Columbia, Maryland, November 6-8, 1995*.

Xueqing Wu, Kung-Hsiang Huang, Yi Fung, and Heng Ji. 2022. Cross-document misinformation detection based on event graph reasoning. In *Proceedings of the 2022 Conference of the North American Chapter of the Association for Computational Linguistics: Human Language Technologies*, pages 543–558.

Carl Yang, Jieyu Zhang, Haonan Wang, Sha Li, Myungwan Kim, Matt Walker, Yiou Xiao, and Jiawei Han. 2020. Relation learning on social networks with multi-modal graph edge variational autoencoders. In *Proceedings of the 13th International Conference on Web Search and Data Mining*, pages 699–707.

A Appendix

Model	Levenshtein Distance (TP)
MP RobBERTje	67.01
MP BERTje (ADPT)	67.23
MP BERTje	68.44
GAE NOFEAT	71.01
GAE BERTje (768)	70.8
GAE BERTje (3072)	70.68
GAE RobBERT (768)	70.57
GAE RobBERT (3072)	70.49
GAE SBERT	70.55
VGAE NOFEAT	69.95
VGAE BERTje (768)	68.71
VGAE BERTje (3072)	70.04
VGAE RobBERT (768)	70.21
VGAE RobBERT (3072)	70.15
VGAE SBERT	70.04

Table 2: Average Levenshtein distance for each True Positive (TP) pair in the test set indicating how well each model predicts comparatively more difficult coreference links.

Model	5	15	25	35	45	55	65	75
MP RobBERTje	0.627	0.631	0.667	0.683	0.701	0.736	0.753	0.766
MP BERTje (ADPT)	0.638	0.640	0.662	0.685	0.692	0.724	0.729	0.754
MP BERTje	0.663	0.675	0.687	0.704	0.721	0.754	0.762	0.781
GAE NOFEAT	0.593	0.667	0.669	0.679	0.747	0.769	0.769	0.786
GAE BERTje (768)	0.736	0.759	0.771	0.789	0.789	0.791	0.815	0.826
GAE BERTje (3072)	0.730	0.756	0.786	0.784	0.805	0.803	0.815	0.849
GAE RobBERT (768)	0.734	0.781	0.771	0.774	0.783	0.791	0.835	0.826
GAE RobBERT (3072)	0.725	0.759	0.788	0.788	0.806	0.810	0.815	0.829
GAE SBERT	0.732	0.768	0.762	0.770	0.762	0.759	0.765	0.786
VGAE NOFEAT	0.632	0.653	0.742	0.752	0.747	0.766	0.781	0.786
VGAE BERTje (768)	0.672	0.747	0.753	0.758	0.758	0.773	0.795	0.809
VGAE BERTje (3072)	0.712	0.769	0.781	0.780	0.776	0.818	0.802	0.818
VGAE RobBERT (768)	0.672	0.745	0.757	0.758	0.759	0.770	0.791	0.799
VGAE RobBERT (3072)	0.691	0.753	0.762	0.764	0.761	0.791	0.800	0.801
VGAE SBERT	0.651	0.681	0.735	0.738	0.726	0.711	0.745	0.735

Table 3: Results (CONLL F1) for the ablation experiments for each individual model. Columns indicate the percentagewise amount of available training data w.r.t the overall size of the ENCORE dataset.

CAW-coref: Conjunction-Aware Word-level Coreference Resolution

Karel D'Oosterlinck[1,*], **Semere Kiros Bitew**[1], **Brandon Papineau**[2]
Christopher Potts[2], **Thomas Demeester**[1], **Chris Develder**[1]
[1]Ghent University – imec [2]Stanford University
*karel.doosterlinck@ugent.be

Abstract

State-of-the-art coreference resolutions systems depend on multiple LLM calls per document and are thus prohibitively expensive for many use cases (e.g., information extraction with large corpora). The leading word-level coreference system (`WL-coref`) attains 96.6% of these SOTA systems' performance while being much more efficient. In this work, we identify a routine yet important failure case of `WL-coref`: dealing with conjoined mentions such as *Tom and Mary*. We offer a simple yet effective solution that improves the performance on the OntoNotes test set by 0.9% F1, shrinking the gap between efficient word-level coreference resolution and expensive SOTA approaches by 34.6%. Our Conjunction-Aware Word-level coreference model (`CAW-coref`) and code is available at `https://github.com/KarelDO/wl-coref`.

1 Introduction

Coreference resolution (or simply *coref*) is the task of clustering mentions in a text, grouping those that refer to the same entity. Coref acts as a fundamental step in many classical NLP pipelines, such as information extraction. Today, however, state-of-the-art (SOTA) coref systems use multiple forward passes of a Large Language model (LLM) *per input document*, making them expensive to train and deploy. This results in limited practical use for classical NLP pipelines, which typically require efficient (and sometimes latency-sensitive) methods.

The most computationally efficient yet competitive neural coref architecture is word-level coref (`WL-coref`; Dobrovolskii, 2021). This method operates by (i) first producing embeddings for each word using one forward pass of a (rather small) LM, then (ii) predicting if pairs of words are coreferent using a lightweight scoring architecture and (iii) finally extracting the spans in the input text associated with these coreferent words. Given a text

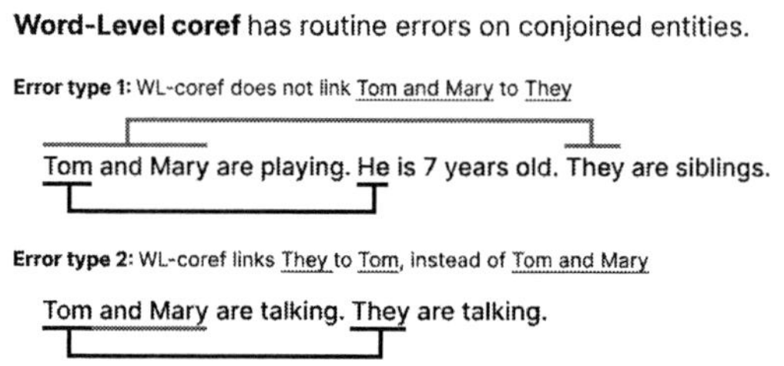

Figure 1: We identify two types of failure cases for `WL-coref` when processing conjoined mentions. Our simple solution, `CAW-coref`, addresses these errors.

of n words, this incurs a computational complexity of $O(n^2)$, since the method operates on pairs of words. However, SOTA methods typically perform *multiple* forward passes of a (Large) LM per input document, making them unwieldy for many practical applications. Furthermore, these techniques suffer both from high infrastructure costs and latency-issues associated with these large models.

While significantly less complex, `WL-coref` attains 96.6% of the performance of the current best coreference model (80.7% F1 out of 83.3% F1)[1], as measured on the English split of the OntoNotes dataset (Pradhan et al., 2012). What makes this even more impressive is that `WL-coref` uses one forward pass of a 355M parameter `roberta-large` encoder (Liu et al., 2019), while the state-of-the-art method (Bohnet et al., 2023) uses multiple forward passes of a 13B parameter `mT5-XXL` model (Xue et al., 2021). Thus, `WL-coref` is the go-to architecture for efficiency-sensitive or long-document coref.

In this work, we describe a fundamental weakness of the `WL-coref` model in its original formulation, stemming from how the word-level coref step

[1]Dobrovolskii (2021) reports a performance of 81.0% F1 for `WL-coref` as best performance on the OntoNotes test set. To avoid selecting the best model on the test set, we instead report the test score achieved by our first rerun of `WL-coref` using their code.

Proceedings of the Sixth Workshop on Computational Models of Reference, Anaphora and Coreference (CRAC 2023), pages 8–14
December 6–7, 2023

was trained. In particular, starting from a dataset that is annotated at the span-level, a word-level dataset is created by using dependency parsing information to select one head-word per span. This causes ambiguity when mentions are conjoined: two spans representing distinct entities can share the same head-word. For example, the span *Tom and Mary* is analyzed as containing three entity mentions (*Tom*, *Mary*, and *Tom and Mary*), and both *Tom and Mary* and *Tom* share the same head-word. When the model at inference time tries to refer both to entity *Tom* and entity *Tom and Mary*, two conflicting links to the span *Tom* are predicted. This causes the model to always drop one of the links, degrading performance (Figure 1).

We resolve this by defining the coordinating conjunction (e.g. *and*, *or*, *plus*) as head-word when faced with these types of mentions, which is a common approach in linguistics (Zoerner III, 1995; Progovac, 1998). Now, the model can learn to systematically link to this conjunction when something is coreferent with *Tom and Mary*, without producing conflicting links. We train a new `WL-coref` model, called Conjunction-Aware Word-level coreference (`CAW-coref`), and find that this simple fix achieves a significant improvement on the OntoNotes test set: the error difference with the state-of-the-art method shrinks by 34.6% (i.e. `CAW-coref` improves the absolute performance of `WL-coref` from 80.7% to 81.6%). Given that this fix incurs no additional model complexity, this gain is an important step forward for efficient coref.

2 Related Work

The main competitive approaches to end-to-end coref can be classified into three broad categories: span-based, word-level, and autoregressive coref.

Span-based coreference Lee et al. (2017) introduce `e2e-coref`, the first end-to-end span-based coref architecture. Starting from word embeddings, the model first predicts which spans are likely a mention. In the second step, coreferent links are predicted between such span-pairs to form coreference clusters. Given a text of n words, this approach incurs $O(n^4)$ computations. Thus, pruning is required to contain the complexity, both for mention prediction and coreference prediction.

Many follow-up works improved upon this architecture by introducing contextualized embeddings (Lee et al., 2018; Kantor and Globerson, 2019), LMs for better span representations (Joshi et al., 2020), ensembling different models for coreference link scoring (`LingMess`; Otmazgin et al., 2023), and distilling the LM backbone for more efficient inference (Otmazgin et al., 2022). Still, the theoretical complexity of these approaches remains $O(n^4)$, requiring pruning and leading to poor scaling on long documents.

Word-level coreference Given an input text, Dobrovolskii (2021) proposes to first predict coreference links between words and subsequently extract the spans surrounding words that are found to be coreferent. This lowers the computational cost of the coref architecture to $O(n^2)$. In turn, less aggressive pruning is needed, which resulted in better performance over conventional span-based techniques.[2] Dobrovolskii (2021) uses one forward pass of a 355M `roberta-large` encoder model to form the contextualized word embeddings needed.

Autoregressive coreference Autoregressive methods iteratively build the coreference structure by running multiple forward passes of an LM backbone. Bohnet et al. (2023) introduce a 13B parameter `mT5-xxl` model called `link-append`: they run multiple forward passes of the LM over increasingly large chunks of the input text and iteratively predict how to grow the coreference structure. This results in the current state-of-the art model on OntoNotes (+2.6% F1 over `WL-coref`). Similarly, Liu et al. (2022) utilize an 11B parameter `Flan-T5-xxl` model (Chung et al., 2022) and predict a sequence of structure-building actions when regressing over the input text (`ASP`). Wu et al. (2020) introduce `corefqa`, formulating coref as a series of question-answering tasks, run multiple forward passes of an LM to build the coreference structure and use extra QA data for augmentation.

In general, the autoregressive methods outperform span-based and word-level coreference, but at great computational cost. All these methods require at least $O(n)$ forward passes of an LM per input document, while span-based or word-level techniques require only one. While some of these computations could be parallelized, running $O(n)$ LM forward passed *per input document* is exceedingly expensive.

Additionally, the `mT5-xxl` and `T0` models used by SOTA methods contain many more parameters

[2] `LingMess` (Otmazgin et al., 2023) is the only span-based method that outperforms `WL-coref`, using a lightweight ensembling technique. This technique could be directly applied to `WL-coref` for potentially a similar performance boost.

compared to the roberta-large model used by WL-coref (13B and 11B respectively, compared to 355M), making these models less accessible to train and deploy. Liu et al. (2022) show that when using an LM comparable in size to the one used by WL-coref, their performance using autoregressive coreference is actually worse. Thus, word-level coreference is the most efficient method in terms of memory requirements and computational scaling.

Error analysis of coreference models Porada et al. (2023) investigate types of errors in recent coref models, including WL-coref. Based on the hypothesis that distinct datasets operationalize the task of coreference differently, they perform generalization experiments between multiple datasets and analyze different types of model error. One of their findings suggests that coref for nested mentions is still hard in general.

In this work, we highlight a failure case of WL-coref, namely, coreference with conjoined entities (i.e. coordinated noun phrases). We propose and empirically validate a simple yet effective solution.

3 The WL-coref model

We briefly summarize the architecture used by Dobrovolskii (2021) and refer to the original publication for a full overview.

Step 1 – Word Representations: First, contextualized word representations are created using one forward pass of an LM backbone and a learned averaging over constituent tokens.

Step 2 – Word-Level Coreference: To create word-level links, a first *coarse antecedent scoring* is constructed between all pairs of words using a learned bilinear function.

For each word, the top k coarse antecedents are considered in a *fine antecedent scoring step*, using a trained feed forward neural network. The final antecedent scores are given by the sum of the coarse and fine scores. These antecedent scores between pairs of words are used to infer the most likely word-level coreference clustering. The words found to be part of a coreference cluster are passed on to Step 3.

Step 3 – Span Extraction: For each coreferent word, the mention span surrounding it is extracted. This is done using a small feed-forward neural network applied to the contextualized word embeddings, followed by a convolutional layer which predicts probabilities for start and end span boundaries. This step is applied individually for each coreferent word and thus is not directly aware of the global clustering produced in Step 2.

Creating word-level data: To train both steps, Dobrovolskii (2021) uses syntactic information to decompose the span-based OntoNotes dataset into a word-level version and a word-to-span dataset.

The crucial step in this decomposition is selecting one head-word per span. Clearly, these head-words need to be as representative as possible of the entity mentioned in the span, so as to allow the word-level linking to perform well. Additionally, the head-words should be systematically picked so that the span extraction step has an easy time learning to extract the correct span surrounding a coreferent head-word.

Dobrovolskii (2021) picks head-words using dependency parsing information already present in the OntoNotes dataset. Given a span, the method selects the head-word as the word in the span which depends on a word outside of the span. If none or multiple of such words are found, the right-most word of the span is selected as head-word.

4 Failure Modes of WL-coref

We describe the two failures cases of WL-coref outlined in Figure 1 and propose a simple solution.

Entity Conjunction: WL-coref is unable to fully solve routine examples where the conjunction of two or more mentions (e.g. via the use of the coordinating conjunction *and*) forms a new mention in the discourse. Consider the first example from Figure 1: *Tom and Mary are playing. He is 7 years old. They are siblings.* Following how head-words were defined in Dobrovolskii 2021, both the head-word for the mention *Tom and Mary* and the mention *Tom* coincide. At inference time, the word-level coreference step will thus predict both the coreferent links *Tom – He* and *Tom – They*. Since the model does not predict a link *He – They*, one of these two predicted links must be dropped in order to arrive at a consistent clustering. Thus, the model is unable to correctly output both coreferent clusters in this trivial example.

Nested Span Extraction: Given a coreferent head-word, WL-coref sometimes struggles to extract the correct span boundaries surrounding this head-word when multiple valid options are possible. Consider the second example from Figure 1: *Tom and Anna are talking. They are talking.* WL-coref

	LM		Link	MUC			B^3			CEAF$_{\phi 4}$			Avg.
	calls	params.	compl.	P	R	F1	P	R	F1	P	R	F1	**F1**
`link-append`	$O(n)$	13B	/	**87.4**	88.3	**87.8**	81.8	**83.4**	**82.6**	79.1	**79.9**	**79.5**	**83.3**
`corefqa`	$O(n^2)$	340M	/	88.6	87.4	88.0	**82.4**	82.0	82.2	**79.9**	78.3	79.1	83.1
`ASP`	$O(n)$	11B	/	86.1	**88.4**	87.2	80.2	83.2	81.7	78.9	78.3	78.6	82.5
`LingMess`	1	355M	$O(n^4)$	85.1	88.1	**86.6**	**78.3**	**82.7**	**80.5**	76.1	78.5	77.3	81.4
`s2e`	1	355M	$O(n^4)$	**85.2**	86.6	85.9	77.9	80.3	79.1	75.4	76.8	76.1	80.3
`CAW` (ours)	1	355M	$O(n^2)$	85.1	**88.2**	**86.6**	77.0	78.0	77.5	**78.0**	**83.2**	**80.6**	**81.6**
`WL`†	1	355M	$O(n^2)$	84.8	87.5	86.1	76.1	76.7	76.6	77.1	82.1	79.5	80.7

Table 1: Results on the OntoNotes 5.0 English test set. Scores calculated with official scorer (Pradhan et al., 2014) or taken from original publication if available. **Avg. F1** is the main metric. We report the amount of LM calls and parameters of the LM used, as well as the coreference linking complexity if applicable. † Dobrovolskii (2021) reports an Avg. F1 of 81.0 as the best `WL-coref` run on the test set, while we report the result of our first run for both `WL-coref` and `CAW-coref`.

correctly predicts the word-level link between *Tom – They*, but fails to extract the span *Tom and Anna* in the subsequent step. This is most likely caused by the span extraction step operating independently on every coreferent head-word: no explicit information about the *Tom – They* link is taken into account when deciding between *Tom* and *Tom and Anna*, and this decision is thus ambiguous.

Proposed Solution: Both failure modes are rooted in the same fundamental problem: there is no unique one-to-one relation between head-words and spans. This causes issues both when predicting word-level links and when performing span extraction, specifically when dealing with nesting.

We propose to solve this by changing how head-words are defined on conjoined mentions. When creating the word-level training data, we use part-of-speech tags supplied in the OntoNotes dataset to detect if a coordinating conjunction (e.g. *and, or, plus*) is present in a span. Then we check the relative depth of the conjunction in the dependency parse of the span. If it is less than two steps away from the head-word of the span, it is selected as new head-word. This selects *and* as head-word in the span *Tom and Ann*, but not in the span *David, whose children are called Tom and Ann*. Thus, we have defined a systematic way of picking head-words for conjoined mentions, in a way that they do not conflict with any of the head-words for the nested mentions.

5 Experiments and Results

We use our new word-level dataset to train `CAW-coref`, a new instance of the `WL-coref` architecture. Using our altered notion of head-words, we train and evaluate this model on the English OntoNotes dataset without changing any hyperparameters compared to the default `WL-coref` run. We immediately find an absolute performance increase of 0.9% F1, setting the performance of `CAW-coref` at 81.6% F1. This shrinks the relative gap between efficient coref and expensive SOTA approaches by 34.6%, which is certainly not trivial since gains on OntoNotes have been hard to come by in recent years.

The full breakdown of the results in function of the official evaluation metrics (Vilain et al., 1995; Bagga and Baldwin, 1998; Luo, 2005; Pradhan et al., 2012) is given in Table 1. `CAW-coref` even outperforms `LingMess`, the best span-based method, which uses ensembling to achieve a significant performance boost. Potentially, such an ensembling technique could be applied to further boost `CAW-coref` performance as well.

In total, we found that 1.17% of spans across the English OntoNotes train and development split were such conjoined entities. Supplementary to our empirical analysis, we show the qualitative improvement of `CAW-coref` on a list of simple examples in Appendix A.

6 Conclusion

Neural coreference resolution techniques should be efficient in order to maximize real-word impact. In this work, we outlined two failure cases of the efficient word-level coreference resolution architecture and addressed them with one simple fix. Our new model, Conjunction-Aware Word-level coreference (`CAW-coref`), shrinks the performance gap between efficient and state-of-the-art coreference by 34.6%, and is currently the most performant efficient neural coreference model.

Limitations

There are always more distinct spans than words in a text, thus it is not always possible to uniquely pick a head-word per span. For example, our proposed solution can't fully handle sequential conjunctions such as *Tom and Mary and David*, since this span contains only 5 words but 6 mentions: *Tom*, *Tom and Mary*, *Mary*, *Mary and David*, and *David*. Luckily, we did not observe any such dense references in the dataset.

Our procedure of selecting a new head-word for conjunctions relies on syntactic information in the form of part-of-speech tags and dependency parses. OntoNotes features several instances where conjunctions are formed using commas or hyphens, such as in the span *Tom , Mary* or *Tom - Mary*. Here, the comma and hyphen should take on the role as head-word of the conjunction, but this is much harder to detect using the syntactic information present.

Future work could focus on resolving both these issues to further boost the performance of efficient Conjunction-Aware Word-level coreference resolution.

Acknowledgements

We are grateful to our anonymous reviewers for their meticulous reading and valuable comments. Karel D'Oosterlinck is funded by an FWO Fundamental Research PhD Fellowship (11632223N).

References

Amit Bagga and Breck Baldwin. 1998. Algorithms for scoring coreference chains.

Bernd Bohnet, Chris Alberti, and Michael Collins. 2023. Coreference resolution through a seq2seq transition-based system. *Transactions of the Association for Computational Linguistics*, 11:212–226.

Hyung Won Chung, Le Hou, Shayne Longpre, Barret Zoph, Yi Tay, William Fedus, Eric Li, Xuezhi Wang, Mostafa Dehghani, Siddhartha Brahma, et al. 2022. Scaling instruction-finetuned language models. *arXiv preprint arXiv:2210.11416*.

Vladimir Dobrovolskii. 2021. Word-level coreference resolution. In *Proceedings of the 2021 Conference on Empirical Methods in Natural Language Processing*, pages 7670–7675, Online and Punta Cana, Dominican Republic. Association for Computational Linguistics.

Mandar Joshi, Danqi Chen, Yinhan Liu, Daniel S. Weld, Luke Zettlemoyer, and Omer Levy. 2020. SpanBERT: Improving pre-training by representing and predicting spans. *Transactions of the Association for Computational Linguistics*, 8:64–77.

Ben Kantor and Amir Globerson. 2019. Coreference resolution with entity equalization. In *Proceedings of the 57th Annual Meeting of the Association for Computational Linguistics*, pages 673–677, Florence, Italy. Association for Computational Linguistics.

Kenton Lee, Luheng He, Mike Lewis, and Luke Zettlemoyer. 2017. End-to-end neural coreference resolution. In *Proceedings of the 2017 Conference on Empirical Methods in Natural Language Processing*, pages 188–197, Copenhagen, Denmark. Association for Computational Linguistics.

Kenton Lee, Luheng He, and Luke Zettlemoyer. 2018. Higher-order coreference resolution with coarse-to-fine inference. In *Proceedings of the 2018 Conference of the North American Chapter of the Association for Computational Linguistics: Human Language Technologies, Volume 2 (Short Papers)*, pages 687–692, New Orleans, Louisiana. Association for Computational Linguistics.

Tianyu Liu, Yuchen Eleanor Jiang, Nicholas Monath, Ryan Cotterell, and Mrinmaya Sachan. 2022. Autoregressive structured prediction with language models. In *Findings of the Association for Computational Linguistics: EMNLP 2022*, pages 993–1005.

Yinhan Liu, Myle Ott, Naman Goyal, Jingfei Du, Mandar Joshi, Danqi Chen, Omer Levy, Mike Lewis, Luke Zettlemoyer, and Veselin Stoyanov. 2019. Roberta: A robustly optimized bert pretraining approach. *arXiv preprint arXiv:1907.11692*.

Xiaoqiang Luo. 2005. On coreference resolution performance metrics. In *Proceedings of Human Language Technology Conference and Conference on Empirical Methods in Natural Language Processing*, pages 25–32, Vancouver, British Columbia, Canada. Association for Computational Linguistics.

Shon Otmazgin, Arie Cattan, and Yoav Goldberg. 2022. F-coref: Fast, accurate and easy to use coreference resolution. In *Proceedings of the 2nd Conference of the Asia-Pacific Chapter of the Association for Computational Linguistics and the 12th International Joint Conference on Natural Language Processing: System Demonstrations*, pages 48–56, Taipei, Taiwan. Association for Computational Linguistics.

Shon Otmazgin, Arie Cattan, and Yoav Goldberg. 2023. Lingmess: Linguistically informed multi expert scorers for coreference resolution. In *Proceedings of the 17th Conference of the European Chapter of the Association for Computational Linguistics*, pages 2744–2752.

Ian Porada, Alexandra Olteanu, Kaheer Suleman, Adam Trischler, and Jackie Chi Kit Cheung. 2023. Investigating failures to generalize for coreference resolution models. *arXiv preprint arXiv:2303.09092*.

Sameer Pradhan, Xiaoqiang Luo, Marta Recasens, Eduard Hovy, Vincent Ng, and Michael Strube. 2014. Scoring coreference partitions of predicted mentions: A reference implementation. In *Proceedings of the 52nd Annual Meeting of the Association for Computational Linguistics (Volume 2: Short Papers)*, pages 30–35, Baltimore, Maryland. Association for Computational Linguistics.

Sameer Pradhan, Alessandro Moschitti, Nianwen Xue, Olga Uryupina, and Yuchen Zhang. 2012. CoNLL-2012 shared task: Modeling multilingual unrestricted coreference in OntoNotes. In *Joint Conference on EMNLP and CoNLL - Shared Task*, pages 1–40, Jeju Island, Korea. Association for Computational Linguistics.

Ljiljana Progovac. 1998. Structure for coordination. *Glot international*, 3(7):3–6.

Marc Vilain, John Burger, John Aberdeen, Dennis Connolly, and Lynette Hirschman. 1995. A model-theoretic coreference scoring scheme. In *Sixth Message Understanding Conference (MUC-6): Proceedings of a Conference Held in Columbia, Maryland, November 6-8, 1995.*

Wei Wu, Fei Wang, Arianna Yuan, Fei Wu, and Jiwei Li. 2020. Corefqa: Coreference resolution as query-based span prediction. In *Proceedings of the 58th Annual Meeting of the Association for Computational Linguistics*, pages 6953–6963.

Linting Xue, Noah Constant, Adam Roberts, Mihir Kale, Rami Al-Rfou, Aditya Siddhant, Aditya Barua, and Colin Raffel. 2021. mT5: A massively multilingual pre-trained text-to-text transformer. In *Proceedings of the 2021 Conference of the North American Chapter of the Association for Computational Linguistics: Human Language Technologies*, pages 483–498, Online. Association for Computational Linguistics.

Cyril Edward Zoerner III. 1995. *Coordination: The syntax of &P.* University of California, Irvine.

Model	Step	Prediction	Correct
WL-coref	word	Tom and Anna are talking. They are talking.	Yes
WL-coref	span	Tom and Anna are talking. They are talking.	No
CAW-coref	word	Tom and Anna are talking. They are talking.	Yes
CAW-coref	span	Tom and Anna are talking. They are talking.	Yes
WL-coref	word	My friend David and my dad Bert are talking. They are talking.	No
WL-coref	span	My friend David and my dad Bert are talking. They are talking.	No
CAW-coref	word	My friend David and my dad Bert are talking. They are talking.	Yes
CAW-coref	span	My friend David and my dad Bert are talking. They are talking.	Yes
WL-coref	word	The Guardian and The Chronicle had a secret meeting . Both newspapers are on thin ice .	No
WL-coref	span	The Guardian and The Chronicle had a secret meeting . Both newspapers are on thin ice .	No
CAW-coref	word	The Guardian and The Chronicle had a secret meeting . Both newspapers are on thin ice .	Yes
CAW-coref	span	The Guardian and The Chronicle had a secret meeting . Both newspapers are on thin ice .	Yes

Table 2: Three hand-crafted examples and their word-level and span-level predictions for WL-coref and CAW-coref. Coreferent predictions are indicated with a colored box, where each unique entity has the same color. Predictions are considered correct or not correct for their respective step in the word-level pipeline.

A Qualitative Examples

Three qualitative examples comparing WL-coref and CAW-coref with the word-level and span-level predictions are given in Table 2.

Towards Transparency in Coreference Resolution: A Quantum-Inspired Approach

Hadi Wazni
University College London
hadi.wazni.20@ucl.ac.uk

Mehrnoosh Sadrzadeh
University College London
m.sadrzade@ucl.ac.uk

Abstract

Guided by grammatical structure, words compose to form sentences, and guided by discourse structure, sentences compose to form dialogues and documents. The compositional aspect of sentence and discourse units is often overlooked by machine learning algorithms. A recent initiative called Quantum Natural Language Processing (QNLP) learns word meanings as points in a Hilbert space and acts on them via a translation of grammatical structure into Parametrised Quantum Circuits (PQCs). Previous work extended the QNLP translation to discourse structure using points in a closure of Hilbert spaces. In this paper, we evaluate this translation on a Winograd-style pronoun resolution task. We train a Variational Quantum Classifier (VQC) for binary classification and implement an end-to-end pronoun resolution system. The simulations executed on IBMQ software converged with an F1 score of 87.20%. The model outperformed two out of three classical coreference resolution systems and neared state-of-the-art SpanBERT. A mixed quantum-classical model yet improved these results with an F1 score increase of around 6%.

1 Introduction

Large language models (LLMs), such as GPT-3 (Brown et al., 2020), have achieved impressive success in various NLP tasks and have become increasingly common in everyday life through search engines, personal assistants, and other applications. They are trained on vast corpora of text, which are sourced from books, articles, and websites. LLMs learn complex connections between words and phrases by predicting the likelihood of a word appearing in the context of other words. These learned probability distributions capture the statistical patterns of word co-occurrences in data; due to this, LLMs are also known as distributional language models.

Despite their successes in advancing language understanding and generation, LLMs often face criticism for being black boxes (Buhrmester et al., 2019). This means that it is challenging to understand how they make their predictions, which can in turn make them unreliable and difficult to debug. One way to enhance the transparency and interpretability of these models is to explicitly integrate linguistic structure (Lambek, 1958; Chomsky, 1957) into them.

A notable approach attempting this integration is the Distributional Compositional Categorical (DisCoCat) model (Coecke et al., 2010; Kartsaklis and Sadrzadeh, 2013), which pioneered the paradigm of merging explicit grammatical (or syntactic) structure with distributional (or statistical) data for encoding and computing meanings of sentences. DisCoCat offered tools for a compositional statistical modelling of sentence-level linguistic phenomena, such as lexical entailment and ambiguity, by providing transparent meaning assignments for complex syntactic structures, e.g. relative and possessive clauses (Sadrzadeh et al., 2013, 2014), conjunctive and negation operations (Lewis, 2020). Its underlying theory, however, relied on generalisations of vectors to higher order tensors, which made the framework in need of large computational resources and led to limited scalability.

Conversely, tensors are natural components of quantum systems, and quantum computing resources can efficiently learn them. This idea has led to the development of Quantum Natural Language Processing (QNLP). In QNLP, words are represented as points within a Hilbert space, grammatical structures are represented as Parameterised Quantum Circuits (PQCs), and the learning of circuit parameters is achieved through simulations conducted on accessible quantum computing resources, such as IBMQ quantum computers. QNLP has so far been applied to a variety of tasks, e.g. sentence classification (Lorenz et al., 2021), sentence generation (Karamlou et al., 2022), question answering (Meichanetzidis et al., 2023), sentiment

Proceedings of the Sixth Workshop on Computational Models of Reference, Anaphora and Coreference (CRAC 2023), pages 15–27
December 6–7, 2023

analysis (Ruskanda et al., 2022; Stein et al., 2023; Ganguly et al., 2023), musical composition (Miranda et al., 2021), and language translation (Abbaszade et al., 2023). Moreover, the theoretical underpinnings of QNLP have been extended to model discourse structure and have been tested on a limited toy dataset (Wazni et al., 2022).

In this paper, we expand this dataset by introducing a few-shot prompting technique and generate synthetic Winograd-style ambiguous coreference sentences (Levesque et al., 2012) using GPT-3. We apply this method to a set of initial sentences from (Rahman and Ng, 2012) and create a dataset consisting of 16,400 entries. This dataset have a larger number of data points, longer and more complex sentences, and a broader range of grammatical structures when compared to the dataset in (Wazni et al., 2022), where sentences followed a subject-verb-object structure.

We train a Variational Quantum Classifier (VQC) for binary classification and integrate it into an end-to-end pronoun resolution system. Our system's performance surpasses that of classical coreference resolution systems such as CoreNLP (Manning et al., 2014) and Neural Coreference (Clark and Manning, 2016a,b), and it achieves results that are close with the state-of-the-art SpanBERT (Lee et al., 2018), with an F1 score of 87.20%. Following recent practice in quantum machine learning (QML) (Araujo and da Silva, 2020; Macaluso et al., 2020), we merge our quantum system with classical engines to construct a *mixed quantum-classical* pronoun resolver. In alignment with results observed in QML across various domains (Grossi et al., 2022; Batra et al., 2020; Kerenidis and Luongo, 2020), we find that the classical and quantum results are *complementary*, thus our mixed approach yields a significant performance improvement, resulting in an approximate 6% increase in the F1 score.

2 Background and Related Work

In the DisCoCat framework, the grammatical structure of a sentence guides the composition of its word-meanings, leading to the derivation of meaning for the sentence as a whole (Coecke et al., 2020, 2013). The grammatical structures are modelled by proofs derived using the rules of Joachim Lambek's logic of syntax, known as the Lambek Calculus (Lambek, 1988). These proofs are interpreted as *processes* and modelled by morphisms of a monoidal category, which comes equipped with a *string diagrammatic* graphical notation (Piedeleu and Zanasi, 2023). Examples of processes that can be effectively modelled by a monoidal category include linear maps over finite-dimensional vector spaces, and this was the initial concept behind the introduction of DisCoCat. Atomic words like noun phrases are represented as points within finite-dimensional vector spaces, while functional words such as adjectives and verbs are depicted as points within the tensor products of these vector spaces. The interconnection of vector and tensor spaces is facilitated through their grammatical dependencies. By contracting these dependencies, the framework allows for the derivation of the overall meaning of the entire sentence.

In fact, the formulation of vectors and tensors into a monoidal category goes back to a framework known as categorical quantum mechanics (CQM), which reformulated quantum theory in terms of process theories and used string diagrams to describe quantum protocols (Abramsky and Coecke, 2008; Coecke and Kissinger, 2017). For a detailed introduction to quantum computing and CQM, see (Nielsen and Chuang, 2010; Coecke and Kissinger, 2017; Sutor, 2019). As a result, monoidal categories and string diagrams became a common base in which one can use analogical reasoning to relate language with quantum theory. For instance, Hilbert spaces, where quantum states are encoded, are vector spaces, so quantum states are related to word-meanings and grammatical reductions correspond to processes such as quantum maps, quantum effects, and measurements.

2.1 Lambek Calculus and its modal extensions

The formulae of *Lambek Calculus* (LC) are generated according to the following BNF:

$$A, B ::= A \in At \mid A \cdot B \mid A \backslash B \mid A / B$$

Atomic types $A \in At$ are atomic linguistic types, e.g. noun phrases n and sentences s, multiplication $A \cdot B$ is their composition, and the slashes $A \backslash B$ and A/B build complex types, e.g. for words with function types such as adjectives and verbs.

In (Kanovich et al., 2020), an extension of LC with two operations $!A$ and ∇A was introduced. The new logic was named *Lambek calculus with soft sub-exponentials* (**SLLM**). In (McPheat et al., 2020), the new modal formulae were used to model the linguistic types found in discourse, e.g. pronouns and other ellipsis markers. The !-modal

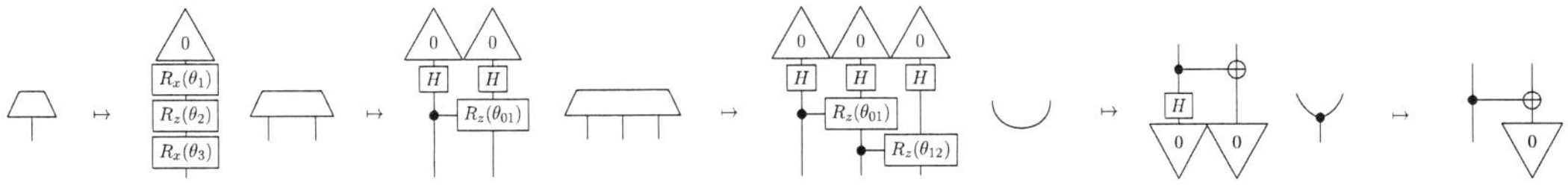

Figure 1: Translation from string diagrams to PQCs using a single-layer IQP ansatz, where each grammatical type is mapped to a 1-qubit space.

types were used for copying referents up to a bound k, and the ∇-modal types moved them to the locations of their markers, where they were referred to. The authors showed how the logic could model and reason about definite pronoun discourse ambiguities, such as the Winograd schema examples, and sloppy vs strict readings of elliptic sentences.

In (Coecke et al., 2013), the following vector space semantics was proposed for LC:

$$[\![A]\!] = V \in FdVect, \qquad [\![A \cdot B]\!] = [\![A]\!] \otimes [\![B]\!]$$

$$[\![A \backslash B]\!] = [\![B/A]\!] = [\![A]\!]^* \otimes [\![B]\!]$$

In this semantics, atomic linguistic types are interpreted as finite-dimensional vector spaces and their multiplication as the tensor product of spaces; the slash types are interpreted as the set of all linear maps between their two spaces, via the dual vector space denoted by $(-)^*$. Words are interpreted as elements of the vector spaces associated to their types. This semantics was extended to **SLLM** in (McPheat et al., 2020), by interpreting the copiable linguistic categories as *k-truncated* Fock spaces, defined as follows:

$$[\![!^k A]\!] = \bigoplus_{i=0}^{k} [\![A]\!]^{\otimes i} = k \oplus [\![A]\!] \oplus ([\![A]\!] \otimes [\![A]\!]) \cdots$$

$$\cdots \oplus ([\![A]\!] \otimes [\![A]\!] \otimes [\![A]\!]) \oplus \cdots \oplus [\![A]\!]^{\otimes k}$$

A Fock space closes its base vector A under an infinite number of tensor products, and a k-truncated version of it only looks at the first k tensors. Access to any copies of a linguistic category (less than the bound k) is facilitated by projecting to that layer. Movable categories take advantage of the commutativity of the tensor product between finite-dimensional vector spaces. The direct sum operation $\oplus$ cannot be directly represented using the quantum gates available in QNLP, which corresponds to the gates provided by IBMQ. We thus translate it into a PQC after projecting it to the desired layer.

A summary of the translation between our Fock space semantics and PQC is provided in Figure 1. Due to space restrictions, we present the translation for the case where only a single qubit is allocated to each atomic linguistic type. In theory, the translation is easily extendible to larger numbers of qubits, but in practice one will face computational limitations. There are two types of diagrams: those on the left, which represent string diagrams associated with vector spaces, and the ones on the right, which depict diagrams used for quantum circuits. On the string diagrammatic side, a parallelogram box with one leg depicts words with an un-copied atomic types. A parallelogram with many legs either depicts a words with a copied type or a functional type. Cupped lines depict the application of a linear map. The concatenation of two atomic sentence types has a conjunctive (rather than tensorial) interpretation, and this is modelled by the Frobenius multiplication between vector spaces. This multiplication is diagrammatically denoted by a bullet symbol (•).

In Figure 2, an example of a string diagram, where *"books"* and *"learning"* are depicted without being copied, which is indicated by their parallelograms having one leg each. *"The students"* is copied and has a parallelogram with two legs. The pronoun *"They"* is shown with one input and one output, giving it two legs. The verbs *"were"* and *"read"* are represented with two inputs and one output, resulting in three legs each. Cupped lines in the diagram illustrate the application of verbs to their subjects and objects, while a bullet symbol (•) is used to connect *"The students read the books"* with *"They were learning"*.

On the circuit side, a triangle labeled with 0 represents a qubit state in the zero computational basis. A box labeled with H signifies a Hadamard gate. A CNOT gate is denoted by a dot connected horizontally to $\oplus$. A controlled-Z-rotation gate with angle α, depicted as a box labeled with $R_\alpha(\theta_i)$, is connected horizontally to a control qubit, where α can be x, y, or z, and θ ranges from 0 to 2π. An upside-down triangle labeled with 0 signifies a measurement in the computational basis, post-selected to be zero.

3 Methodology

We build upon the steps in (Lorenz et al., 2021) to represent an entire discourse as a PQC.

Parsing and Diagram Generation: The first step involves parsing a discourse into a proof in **SLLM**. We do this via a translation to Combinatory Categorial Grammar (CCG)[1], which enables the use of the state-of-the-art parser (Clark, 2021; Yeung and Kartsaklis, 2021). The parse trees are then transformed to string diagrams through *DisCoPy* (de Felice et al., 2021).

Diagram Optimisation: The number of qubits available on contemporary quantum computers is restricted. For instance, IBM's largest superconducting quantum computer, as of now, has a maximum of 433 qubits[2]. Publicly accessible devices typically offer fewer qubits, often less than 10. Consequently, in the second step, the string diagrams are optimised to minimise the number of qubits associated to them after the translation. QNLP diagrams are composed of a layer of tensors, followed by a layer of applications between the tensors. One approach to reduce the number of qubits is elimination of cups through the transformation of states into effects. Another approaches aims for stretching and reordering them. *Lambeq* (Kartsaklis et al., 2021a) supports additional rewriting rules. An example of an optimised diagram is provided in Figure 2.

Quantum Circuit Transformation: In the last step, the optimised string diagrams are transformed into quantum circuits. This conversion relies on a parameterisation scheme, known as an *ansatz*. An *ansatz* serves as a mapping that determines the quantity of qubits linked with each wire in the string diagram, along with a distinct variational quantum circuit associated with each word. In this study, we choose the popular *Instantaneous Quantum Polynomial* (IQP) ansatz, developped in (Shepherd and Bremner, 2009; Havlíček et al., 2019). The resulting quantum circuits are ready for execution on either a quantum computer or a simulator. The details of training these circuits can be found in Section 4.3. Figure 3 illustrates the circuit derived from the diagram presented in Figure 2.

[1]A grammar formalism inspired by combinatory logic and developed in (Steedman, 2001)

[2]https://www.ibm.com/quantum/roadmap

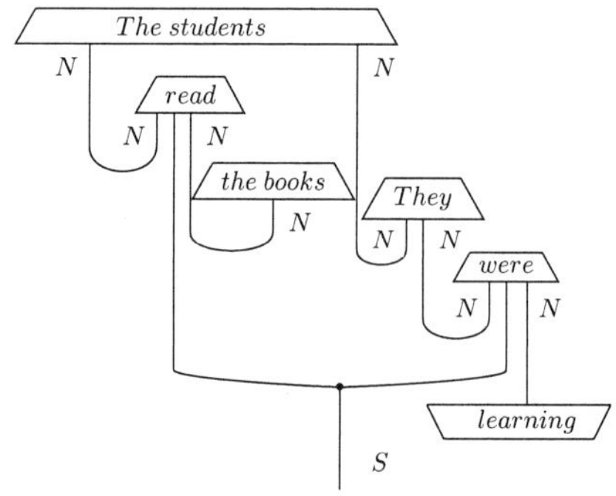

Figure 2: An optimized **SLLM** diagram for a pair of sentences *"The students read the books. They were learning."* To enhance clarity, we treat the determiner-noun phrases *"The students"* and *"The books"* as single units, as determiners are eventually discarded in the rewriting process.

4 Classification Task

Pronoun resolution is a computational linguistic process that involves identifying the antecedent of a pronoun within a text. In our experiment, we consider pronoun resolution as a supervised binary classification task. Given a sentence containing a pronoun, the goal is to determine whether a potential antecedent (such as a noun or noun phrase) in the preceding sentence is the correct referent for the pronoun or not. This task requires training a variational quantum classifier with labeled data, where each pronoun-noun pair is classified as *non-coreferent* or *coreferent*. The code and data used in this paper are available at the following link: `https://github.com/hwazni/Qcoref`

4.1 Dataset

The process of training PQCs involves optimising multiple parameters associated with each word in a given dataset, with the objective of minimising the loss value on the training set. When it comes to predicting the output for a test sample, a PQC is constructed based on the input sentence. Each word in the sentence is associated with a specific set of parameters learned during the training process. A significant challenge arises when an out-of-vocabulary word is encountered during inference, which includes testing or using the model for predictions. These words lack a predefined parameter assignment. To address this issue, there are several approaches, including random initialisation, replacement with a special token like "UNK" for

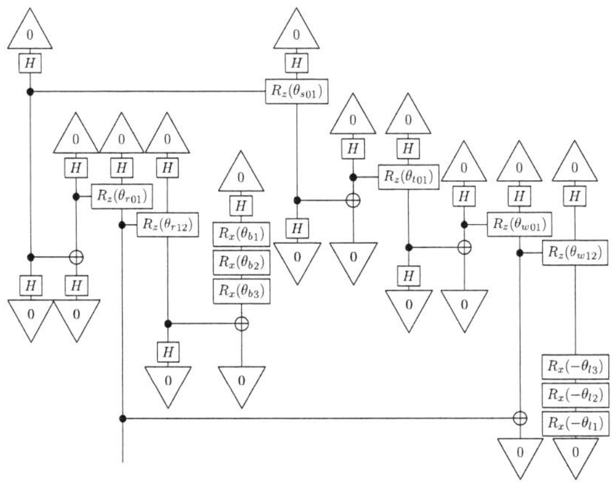

Figure 3: A PQC using the IQP ansatz, transformed from the string diagram presented in Figure 2. The parameters $\{\theta_{s01}\}$, $\{\theta_{r01}, \theta_{r12}\}$, and $\{\theta_{b1}, \theta_{b2}, \theta_{b3}\}$ are associated with the terms *the students*, *read*, and *the books* respectively, while $\{\theta_{t01}\}$, $\{\theta_{w01}, \theta_{w12}\}$ and $\{-\theta_{l3}, -\theta_{l2}, -\theta_{l1}\}$ are associated with *They*, *were*, and *learning* respectively.

unknown words, or establishing an overlap between the test and training vocabularies. In our case, we fix a set of words with grammatical relations between them, then use these and prompt the GPT-3 model to generate pairs of sentences that exhibit a substantial overlap in vocabulary.

In the initial step, we selected entries from the definite pronoun resolution dataset introduced in (Rahman and Ng, 2012), an extension of the Winograd Schema Challenge dataset (Levesque et al., 2012). We excluded sentences containing proper nouns and negation, and gave preference to shorter sentences. This process resulted in a total of 10 entries. Each entry was a pair of sentences. The first sentence, exemplified by E_1 : *The students read the books*, contains two referent nouns, namely, *the students* and *the books*. In the second sentence, an ambiguous pronoun is introduced, referring to one of the referents in E_1. For instance, it could be either E_2 : *They were learning* or *They were interesting*. Notably, the pronoun aligns with gender, number, and semantic class concerning each of the candidate referents mentioned in the first sentence. For each initially selected pair (E_1, E_2), we created an additional set of pairs (S_1, S_2) incorporating a more diverse range of grammatical structures. In these template pairs, S_1 retained the same referents as E_1, and S_2 maintained the same co-reference relation with E_1. Below is the list of template pairs for the *student-book* example.

1. The students *(verb, phrasal verb, verb phrase)* the books. They were *(adjective, gerund phrase)*.
2. The *(adjective)* students *(verb, phrasal verb, verb phrase)* the books. They were *(adjective, gerund phrase)*.
3. The students *(verb, phrasal verb, verb phrase)* the *(adjective)* books. They were *(adjective, gerund phrase)*.
4. The *(adjective)* students *(verb, phrasal verb, verb phrase)* the *(adjective)* books. They were *(adjective, gerund phrase)*.

The templates replace the verb *"read"* by another *verb*, *phrasal verb* or a *verb phrase*. Similarly, the adjectives *"learning"* and *"interesting"* can be replaced by another *adjective* or *gerund phrase*. Sample templates for different examples are listed in section 5.4.

Next, we utilize the prompt provided in the box below in GPT-3 along with template pairs. This technique referred as few-shot prompting, where we provide examples in the prompt to steer the model to better performance (Brown et al., 2020; Kaplan et al., 2020; Touvron et al., 2023). Note that the red tokens are modified for each example.

Provide alternative sentences by replacing the words or phrases inside the brackets for each statement. Utilize different verbs, phrasal verbs, verb phrases, adjectives, or gerund phrases to create new sentences based on the given structure. Ensure that the pronoun 'they' in the second sentence refers to 'students' / Ensure that the pronoun 'they' in the second sentence refers to 'books'

From the GPT-generated output, we eliminated incorrect referent sentences and duplicate examples, retaining only well-formed sentences that possess meaningful content. We carefully handpicked between 300 to 400 examples for each entry, ensuring a balanced distribution of pronoun references. Then we used the generated linguistic elements, including *verbs, phrasal verbs, adjectives, adverbs, nouns, compound nouns, verb phrases, adverbial phrases, gerund phrases, and prepositional phrases*, with 8 distinct structural patterns to generate over 8 million diverse combinations. We randomly choose 1800 pairs for each example, with one example with 200 pairs. This ended

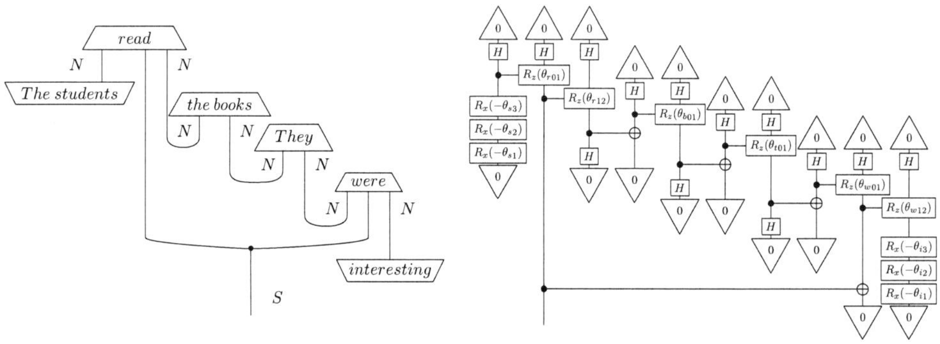

Figure 4: An optimised **SLLM** diagram where the pronoun refers to the object: *"The students read the books. They were interesting."* The diagram along with its transformation into a PQC.

Sentence Pair (S_1, S_2)	**Pronoun**	**Noun**	**Label**
The students researched the books. They were seeking new insights.	They	students	1
The massive storm cancelled the flight. It was full of passengers.	It	storm	0
The precise sniper eliminated the ruthless terrorist. He was a vicious dealer.	He	terrorist	1
The exhausted sailors threw themselves off the boats. They were in poor condition.	They	sailors	0

Table 1: Dataset entries: each sentence pair is labeled with a "0" signifying that the pronoun do not refer to the candidate noun. Conversely, a "1" label indicates that the pronoun and the noun are co-referential.

up with 16,400 (0.2%) examples, comprising approximately 200,000 words, with 1,214 unique vocabulary. Through this approach, we achieved the generation of coherent sentences that uphold grammatical correctness and preserve semantic consistency, as a result a high quality was ensured for the dataset. The dataset was subsequently split into three subsets: 10,496 pairs (~60%) for training, 2,624 pairs (~20%) for validation, and 3,280 pairs (~20%) for testing. The training and testing datasets share a common vocabulary of 95%, while none of the sentence pairs in the testing set appears in the training or validation sets. Some examples of the dataset are provided in Table 1.

4.2 Simulating the quantum circuits

Computation using currently available quantum computers, which are called NISQ for Noisy Intermediate-Scale Quantum, is slow, noisy and limited. They lack the practicality needed for extensive training and comprehensive comparative analyses (Preskill, 2018). For this reason, and especially at the early stages of modelling, proofs-of-concept are obtained by running simulations. A simple way to simulate a quantum computation is to use linear algebra; since quantum gates correspond to complex-valued tensors, each circuit can be represented as a tensor network where computation takes place as a result of a series of tensor contractions. The output of these contractions is the ideal probability distribution of the measurement outcomes on a noise-free quantum computer, i.e. an idealistic approximation of the sampled probability distribution obtained from a NISQ device. We conduct our experiments using noiseless non-shot-based simulations utilizing the *NumPyModel* of *Lambeq* (Kartsaklis et al., 2021b) with a JAX backend (Frostig et al., 2018).

4.3 Training

We implement a hybrid classical-quantum training approach in which the quantum computer is responsible for computing the meaning of the sentence by connecting the quantum states in a quantum circuit and the classical computer is used to calculate the training's loss function. During each iteration, a new set of quantum states is generated, driven by the loss function's outcome from the preceding iteration. This iterative procedure ensures that the quantum states are continually refined to enhance the model's performance and accuracy.

Specifically, the sentence pair (S_1, S_2) within each dataset entry are combined to create a single output quantum state. These resultant states are the inputs to our binary classifier. In principle, they can be any quantum map that take two sentences as input and produce a sentence as the output (recall the whole circuit is represented by an open sentence wire). A CNOT gate is used to combine the two sentences, as it encodes a commutative Frobenius multiplication ($\bullet$) and acts similar to a logical conjunction. The resulting quantum circuit is denoted by $S_1 \bullet S_2$ and evaluated for an initial set of parameters $\Theta = (\theta_1, \theta_2, ..., \theta_k)$ on a quantum computer giving an output state $|S_1 \bullet S_2\,(\Theta)\rangle$. The expected prediction is given by the Born rule, i.e. as follows:

$$l^i_\Theta(S_1 \bullet S_2) := |\langle i|S_1 \bullet S_2(\Theta)\rangle|^2 + \epsilon$$

where, $i \in \{0, 1\}$, ϵ is a smoothing term with the value 10^{-9}, and $l_\Theta(S_1 \bullet S_2)$ is the following probability distribution:

$$l_\Theta(S_1 \bullet S_2) := \frac{(l^0_\Theta(S_1 \bullet S_2), l^1_\Theta(S_1 \bullet S_2))}{\sum_i l^i_\Theta(S_1 \bullet S_2)}$$

The predicted label is obtained by rounding the probability distribution to the nearest integer $\lfloor l_\Theta(S_1 \bullet S_2)\rceil$ and represented as one-hot encoding. This means if $\lfloor l_\Theta(S_1 \bullet S_2)\rceil < 0.5$, the predicted label $[0, 1]$ corresponds to *non-coreferent* mentions, and if $\lfloor l_\Theta(S_1 \bullet S_2)\rceil \geq 0.5$, the predicted label $[1, 0]$ corresponds to *coreferent* mentions.

To find the optimal parameters for our model, the predicted label is compared with the training label using a binary cross-entropy loss function and minimised using a non-gradient-based optimisation algorithm known as SPSA (Simultaneous Perturbation Stochastic Approximation) (Spall, 1998).

For the hyper-parameters, we set the initial learning rate *a* to 0.1, the initial parameter-shift scaling *c* to 0.06, and the stability constant *A* to 20. We run for 2000 epochs of SPSA during which we evaluate the training loss and accuracy. This process is repeated 15 times with random seed values. This is essential since the gradient computed by the SPSA procedure is an approximation and the performance in QML is known to be very sensitive to the initial parameter assignment (Holmes et al., 2022; Grant et al., 2019; McClean et al., 2018).

5 Results and Discussion

5.1 Quantum Approaches: SLLM vs Bag-of-Words

The graphs in Figure 5 illustrate how the models converged smoothly. Across different runs, a common trend emerges—training loss decreases and training accuracy increases steadily. Initially, the average training loss is 1.144, which drops to 0.483 after 2000 iterations. Minimum and maximum values range from 0.369 to 0.571 for different runs. Similarly, the average training accuracy starts at 0.514 and ends at 0.752 after 2000 iterations. The highest recorded accuracy is 0.827, and the lowest is 0.682 amongst all the runs. The testing accuracy rates vary between 0.628 and 0.782, averaging around 0.70. These results demonstrate that the model is able to generalise its predictions beyond training, with well-balanced performance levels.

To understand whether the promising performance of the **SLLM** classifier is due to the structural symbolic type-driven representations or the use of PQCs, we conducted a comparative analysis with quantum circuits generated from a simple bag-of-words diagram (see section 5.4). In this approach, each word is represented with a single qubit, regardless of its grammatical type (e.g., noun, adjective, or verb). Consequently, this model disregards sentence structure and connects all qubits using CNOT gates (the simplest counterparts to addition in quantum circuits). We trained the model under identical hyper-parameters and the same number of training runs. However, its performance fell short, yielding an average testing accuracy of 0.557.

5.2 Classical Approaches: SVM, CoreNLP, Neural Coreference, SpanBERT

We implemented a Support Vector Machine (SVM) for a binary classification task and evaluated its performance in comparison to our VQC. The inputs to the SVM were pre-trained Sentence-BERT embeddings (Reimers and Gurevych, 2019), one per each dataset entry. We also experimented with a compositional model, by adding SBERT word embeddings of each entry, as shown below:

SVM Full : $\vec{E}$
SVM Add : $(\vec{w_1} + \vec{w_2} + \vec{w_3}...) + (\vec{w_1} + \vec{w_4} + \vec{w_5}...)$

In the above, E is an entry such as: *"The students researched the books. The students were seeking*

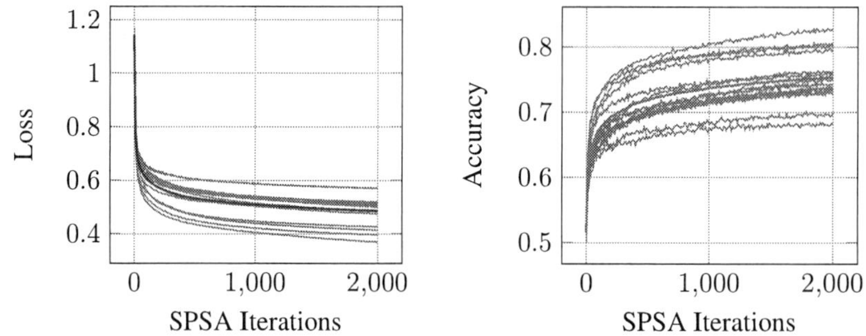

Figure 5: Performance of 15 different runs of a classical simulation of the training set showing the average training loss (blue) and the average training accuracy (red).

new insights." labeled as 1 or *"The massive storm cancelled the flight. The storm was full of passengers."* labeled as 0. In **SVM Add**, $\overrightarrow{w_1}$ is a candidate referent, e.g. *students* or *storm*, and $\overrightarrow{w_2}$, $\overrightarrow{w_3}$, $\overrightarrow{w_4}$, $\overrightarrow{w_5}$ are all the other words.

The objective here was to assess the discourse relation within each entry. We achieved this objective by replacing the pronoun with either the correct or the incorrect referent, thereby evaluating the the discourse relation between them. The training process involved optimising two hyper-parameters: the regularisation parameter c and the choice of kernel type, which could be either linear or a radial basis function (RBF). We leveraged a grid search technique with a 10 fold cross-validation scheme to identify the most suitable combination of hyper-parameters. The resulting SVM model with the best-tuned hyper-parameters was used for evaluation on the testing dataset. The results in Table 2 show that **SVM Add** achieved a lower F1 score of 0.821 in comparison to **SVM Full**, which achieved a solid F1 score of 0.914.

Model	**F1 Score**
SVM Full	0.914
SVM Add	0.821

Table 2: Evaluation performance of classical compositional and non-compositional SVM models

Additionally, we evaluated CoreNLP (Manning et al., 2014), Neural Coreference (Clark and Manning, 2016a) (Clark and Manning, 2016b), and SpanBERT (Lee et al., 2018). CoreNLP combines rule-based techniques with statistical models to resolve coreference; Neural Coreference employs deep learning to capture patterns and dependencies in text, and SpanBERT is a specialised version of BERT (Devlin et al., 2019) fine-tuned for coreference resolution. We ran the pre-trained models using Stanza[3], HuggingFace[4], and AllenNLP[5] libraries respectively. The outcomes are presented in Table 3.

Model	**F1 Score**
CoreNLP	0.563
Neural Coreference	0.585
SpanBERT	**0.927**
QuantumCoref	0.872

Table 3: Evaluation performance of classical neural models

The performance levels amongst these systems were diverse. CoreNLP achieved the lowest F1 score of 0.563, while SpanBERT demonstrated the highest score of 0.927. Neural Coreference achieved a moderate score of 0.585, trailing behind SpanBERT but outperforming CoreNLP.

To facilitate the use of our approach, we implemented an end-to-end system named *QuantumCoref* that consists of two sub-modules: (a) a mentions-detection module that uses SpaCy's[6] part-of-speech parser to identify a set of potential coreference mentions, and (b) our highest-accurate trained **SLLM** classifier, which computes coreference scores for each pair of potential mentions. It achieved an F1 score of 0.872 near SpanBERT.

5.3 Mixed Quantum + Classical Models

To maximize the strengths of quantum and classical systems, we combine their predictions in the following manner: when a classical system predicts an incorrect referent, we opt for the prediction of

[3]https://corenlp.run/
[4]https://huggingface.co/coref/
[5]https://demo.allennlp.org/coreference-resolution/
[6]https://spacy.io/usage/linguistic-features

Model	F1 Score
CoreNLP + QuantumCoref	0.930
Neural Coreference + QuantumCoref	0.946
SpanBERT+ QuantumCoref	**0.986**
SVM Full + QuantumCoref	0.959
SVM Add + QuantumCoref	0.910

Table 4: Evaluation performance of mixed quantum + classical models

QuantumCoref. Similarly, when a classical model fails to identify a referent, resulting in an empty cluster, we rely on *QuantumCoref* for classification. As an example, consider the discourse *"The students learned from the books. They were filled with knowledge."* In this scenario, while SpanBERT detected that the pronoun *"they"* refers to *"students"*, *QuantumCoref* correctly identified the coreference relationship as *"they-books"*. As a result, this mixed quantum-classical approach recognised *"they"* and *"books"* as co-referent entities. By combining the two approaches, we were able to extract the best outcomes from each model, thus enhancing the overall performance. CoreNLP improved from 0.563 to 0.930, Neural Coreference from 0.585 to 0.946, and SpanBERT from 0.927 to 0.986. The SVM models reacted in a similar fashion: the performance of SVM Add increased from 0.821 to 0.910 and that of SVM Full from 0.914 to 0.959.

5.4 Discussion

In a more detailed analysis, among the incorrect predictions, SpanBERT identified pronouns referring to the first noun in 95% of the cases and to the second noun in 5% of the cases. This highlights how SpanBERT struggles in identifying the correct referent, particularly when it's positioned towards the end of the sentence, leading to a higher preference for selecting the first noun.

In situations characterised by linguistic ambiguities, SpanBERT struggles in recognising referential connections. Notably, in instances where multiple plausible nouns could serve as antecedents for pronouns, SpanBERT returns an empty cluster. For instance, in *"The productive bee flew over the flower. It was magnificent."* the complexity arises from the fact that both *"productive bee"* and *"flower"* are reasonable candidates for the antecedent. Similarly, in *"The sailors jumped from the boats. They were having technical problems."*, the ambiguity arises from the potential referents for the pronoun *"They"* which could be either the *"sailors"* or the *"boats"*. In contrast, *QuantumCoref* relies on sentence structure and the connections between entities and their referents. Impressively, *QuantumCoref* solves 319 examples where SpanBERT misclassified, showcasing a success rate of 81.37% and handled 35 examples where SpanBERT returned empty clusters, with a success rate of 68.62%. When our dataset was converted into CoNLL format and SpanBERT was fine-tuned on it, unsurprisingly, it achieved an F1 score of 0.998.

We would like to emphasise that these experiments were not specifically aimed at showcasing *quantum advantage* over classical coreference resolution systems. Our aim was to demonstrate the capabilities of our quantum-based approach, which also offers transparency. Furthermore, SpanBERT, with its exceptional coreference resolution capabilities, requires high computational resources. The fine-tuned SpanBERT model comprises a total of 366 million parameters, which is substantially larger compared to *QuantumCoref*, with a total of 2693 parameters. This highlights the efficiency of the quantum-based approach. There is potential for further improvements, especially when a greater number of qubits are used in modelling. Our setting can resolve general coreference relations in the same way as anaphoric ones. When multiple expressions co-refer, the main entity becomes a Fock space and the rest are pronoun types. We leave experimentation in this direction to future work.

Limitations

We classify the limitations into the following items:

- **Syntax.** It would be tempting to call **SLLM**, the logic of discourse. It, however, does not have a connective for conjoining sentences. In this paper, we resolved the problem in the semantics, by using the Frobenius multiplication for conjoining sentences. A better logic for discourse should include this connective in its syntax.

- **Semantics.** The vector space semantics of $\mathbf{SLLM}$ over unifies the types, e.g. its copiable and functional types are assigned the same vector space semantics, e.g. two copies of a noun phrase and an adjective both have the same $[\![N \otimes N]\!]$ semantics.

- **Automated Parsing.** $\mathbf{SLLM}$ does not have an automatic parser and at the moment its use implies manual type annotations to words. LC has an automatic parser that can be extended to the new types introduced in $\mathbf{SLLM}$. An automatic learning procedure for types, however, requires a corpus annotated with $\mathbf{SLLM}$ types. At this stage, we foresee any co-reference annotated corpus can easily be transferred to an $\mathbf{SLLM}$ annotated one.

- **Quantum Computation.** We relied on simulations for training circuit parameters instead of using real quantum computers. Currently, we are experimenting with a shot-based simulation with an incorporated noise model. This approach takes into consideration critical factors such as quantum gate errors, decoherence, and shot noise, all of which affect practical quantum computing. It can be ported for execution on a quantum computer.

- **Different Types of Anaphora.** In this paper, we focused on definite pronoun resolution and identity anaphora. Non-definite and non-identity anaphora cases, such as bridging and event anaphora, pose challenges and require further theoretical work.

- **OntoNotes.** Our original goal was to run the model on OntoNotes. This turned out to be impossible due to two main reasons. One was that we needed a large overlap between the vocabularies used in training and testing. Secondly, the entries of OntoNotes consist of long complex sentences, which would lead to large quantum circuits. These could not even be efficiently simulated with the current technology.

Acknowledgement

The authors gratefully acknowledge the three anonymous reviewers for their valuable comments. Mehrnoosh Sadrzadeh is grateful to the Royal Academy of Engineering Research Chair/Senior Research Fellowship RCSRF2122-14-152 on Engineered Mathematics for Modelling Typed Structures. Hadi Wazni would like to express gratitude for support by UCL CS department for the PhD scholarships. Both authors would like to thank Lo Ian Kin for many helpful discussions and some help in implmentation.

References

Mina Abbaszade, Mariam Zomorodi, Vahid Salari, and Philip Kurian. 2023. Toward quantum machine translation of syntactically distinct languages.

Samson Abramsky and Bob Coecke. 2008. Categorical quantum mechanics.

Ismael C. S. Araujo and Adenilton J. da Silva. 2020. Quantum ensemble of trained classifiers. In *2020 International Joint Conference on Neural Networks (IJCNN)*, pages 1–8.

Kushal Batra, Kimberley M. Zorn, Daniel H. Foil, Eni Minerali, Victor O. Gawriljuk, Thomas R. Lane, and sean ekins. 2020. Quantum machine learning for drug discovery. *ChemRxiv*.

Tom B. Brown, Benjamin Mann, Nick Ryder, Melanie Subbiah, Jared Kaplan, Prafulla Dhariwal, Arvind Neelakantan, Pranav Shyam, Girish Sastry, Amanda Askell, Sandhini Agarwal, Ariel Herbert-Voss, Gretchen Krueger, Tom Henighan, Rewon Child, Aditya Ramesh, Daniel M. Ziegler, Jeffrey Wu, Clemens Winter, Christopher Hesse, Mark Chen, Eric Sigler, Mateusz Litwin, Scott Gray, Benjamin Chess, Jack Clark, Christopher Berner, Sam McCandlish, Alec Radford, Ilya Sutskever, and Dario Amodei. 2020. Language models are few-shot learners.

Vanessa Buhrmester, David Münch, and Michael Arens. 2019. Analysis of explainers of black box deep neural networks for computer vision: A survey.

Noam Chomsky. 1957. *Syntactic Structures*. Mouton and Co., The Hague.

Kevin Clark and Christopher D. Manning. 2016a. Deep reinforcement learning for mention-ranking coreference models. In *Proceedings of the 2016 Conference on Empirical Methods in Natural Language Processing*, pages 2256–2262, Austin, Texas. Association for Computational Linguistics.

Kevin Clark and Christopher D. Manning. 2016b. Improving coreference resolution by learning entity-level distributed representations. In *Proceedings of the 54th Annual Meeting of the Association for Computational Linguistics (Volume 1: Long Papers)*, pages 643–653, Berlin, Germany. Association for Computational Linguistics.

Stephen Clark. 2021. Something old, something new: Grammar-based ccg parsing with transformer models.

B. Coecke, M. Sadrzadeh, and S. Clark. 2010. Mathematical Foundations for Distributed Compositional Model of Meaning. Lambek Festschrift. *Linguistic Analysis*, 36:345–384.

Bob Coecke, Giovanni de Felice, Konstantinos Meichanetzidis, and Alexis Toumi. 2020. Foundations for near-term quantum natural language processing.

Bob Coecke, Edward Grefenstette, and Mehrnoosh Sadrzadeh. 2013. Lambek vs. lambek: Functorial vector space semantics and string diagrams for lambek calculus. *Ann. Pure and Applied Logic*, 164:1079 – 1100.

Bob Coecke and Aleks Kissinger. 2017. *Picturing Quantum Processes: A First Course in Quantum Theory and Diagrammatic Reasoning*. Cambridge University Press.

Giovanni de Felice, Alexis Toumi, and Bob Coecke. 2021. DisCoPy: Monoidal categories in python. *Electronic Proceedings in Theoretical Computer Science*, 333:183–197.

Jacob Devlin, Ming-Wei Chang, Kenton Lee, and Kristina Toutanova. 2019. Bert: Pre-training of deep bidirectional transformers for language understanding.

Roy Frostig, Matthew Johnson, and Chris Leary. 2018. Compiling machine learning programs via high-level tracing.

Srinjoy Ganguly, Sai Nandan Morapakula, and Luis Miguel Pozo Coronado. 2023. Quantum natural language processing based sentiment analysis using lambeq toolkit.

Edward Grant, Leonard Wossnig, Mateusz Ostaszewski, and Marcello Benedetti. 2019. An initialization strategy for addressing barren plateaus in parametrized quantum circuits. *Quantum*, 3:214.

M. Grossi, N. Ibrahim, V. Radescu, R. Loredo, K. Voigt, C. von Altrock, and A. Rudnik. 2022. Mixed quantum–classical method for fraud detection with quantum feature selection. *IEEE Transactions on Quantum Engineering*, 3(01):1–12.

Vojtěch Havlíček, Antonio D. Córcoles, Kristan Temme, Aram W. Harrow, Abhinav Kandala, Jerry M. Chow, and Jay M. Gambetta. 2019. Supervised learning with quantum-enhanced feature spaces. *Nature*, 567(7747):209–212.

Zoë Holmes, Kunal Sharma, M. Cerezo, and Patrick J. Coles. 2022. Connecting ansatz expressibility to gradient magnitudes and barren plateaus. *PRX Quantum*, 3:010313.

M. Kanovich, S. Kuznetsov, V. Nigam, and A. Scedrov. 2020. Soft Subexponentials and Multiplexing. In *Lecture Notes in Computer Science (including subseries Lecture Notes in Artificial Intelligence and Lecture Notes in Bioinformatics)*.

Jared Kaplan, Sam McCandlish, Tom Henighan, Tom B. Brown, Benjamin Chess, Rewon Child, Scott Gray, Alec Radford, Jeffrey Wu, and Dario Amodei. 2020. Scaling laws for neural language models.

Amin Karamlou, Marcel Pfaffhauser, and James Wootton. 2022. Quantum natural language generation on near-term devices.

D. Kartsaklis and M. Sadrzadeh. 2013. Prior disambiguation of word tensors for constructing sentence vectors. In *Proceedings of the 2013 Conference on Empirical Methods in Natural Language Processing*, pages 1590–1601.

Dimitri Kartsaklis, Ian Fan, Richie Yeung, Anna Pearson, Robin Lorenz, Alexis Toumi, Giovanni de Felice, Konstantinos Meichanetzidis, Stephen Clark, and Bob Coecke. 2021a. lambeq: An efficient high-level python library for quantum nlp.

Dimitri Kartsaklis, Ian Fan, Richie Yeung, Anna Pearson, Robin Lorenz, Alexis Toumi, Giovanni de Felice, Konstantinos Meichanetzidis, Stephen Clark, and Bob Coecke. 2021b. lambeq: An Efficient High-Level Python Library for Quantum NLP. *arXiv preprint arXiv:2110.04236*.

Iordanis Kerenidis and Alessandro Luongo. 2020. Classification of the mnist data set with quantum slow feature analysis. *Phys. Rev. A*, 101:062327.

J. Lambek. 1988. *Categorial and Categorical Grammars*, pages 297–317. Springer Netherlands, Dordrecht.

Joachim Lambek. 1958. The mathematics of sentence structure. *The American Mathematical Monthly*, 65(3):154–170.

Kenton Lee, Luheng He, and Luke Zettlemoyer. 2018. Higher-order coreference resolution with coarse-to-fine inference. In *Proceedings of the 2018 Conference of the North American Chapter of the Association for Computational Linguistics: Human Language Technologies, Volume 2 (Short Papers)*, pages 687–692, New Orleans, Louisiana. Association for Computational Linguistics.

Hector J. Levesque, Ernest Davis, and Leora Morgenstern. 2012. The winograd schema challenge. In *Proceedings of the International Workshop on Temporal Representation and Reasoning*.

Martha Lewis. 2020. Towards logical negation for compositional distributional semantics.

Robin Lorenz, Anna Pearson, Konstantinos Meichanetzidis, Dimitri Kartsaklis, and Bob Coecke. 2021. Qnlp in practice: Running compositional models of meaning on a quantum computer.

Antonio Macaluso, Luca Clissa, Stefano Lodi, and Claudio Sartori. 2020. Quantum Ensemble for Classification.

Christopher Manning, Mihai Surdeanu, John Bauer, Jenny Finkel, Steven Bethard, and David McClosky. 2014. The Stanford CoreNLP natural language processing toolkit. In *Proceedings of 52nd Annual Meeting of the Association for Computational Linguistics: System Demonstrations*, pages 55–60, Baltimore, Maryland. Association for Computational Linguistics.

Jarrod R. McClean, Sergio Boixo, Vadim N. Smelyanskiy, Ryan Babbush, and Hartmut Neven. 2018. Barren plateaus in quantum neural network training landscapes. *Nature Communications*, 9(1).

L. McPheat, H. Wazni, and M. Sadrzadeh. 2020. Vector space semantics for lambek calculus with soft subexponentials. In *Proceedings of the tenth international conference on Logical Aspect of Computational Linguistics*.

Konstantinos Meichanetzidis, Alexis Toumi, Giovanni de Felice, and Bob Coecke. 2023. Grammar-aware sentence classification on quantum computers. *Quantum Machine Intelligence*, 5(1).

Eduardo Reck Miranda, Richie Yeung, Anna Pearson, Konstantinos Meichanetzidis, and Bob Coecke. 2021. A quantum natural language processing approach to musical intelligence.

Michael A. Nielsen and Isaac L. Chuang. 2010. *Quantum Computation and Quantum Information: 10th Anniversary Edition*. Cambridge University Press.

Robin Piedeleu and Fabio Zanasi. 2023. An introduction to string diagrams for computer scientists.

John Preskill. 2018. Quantum computing in the NISQ era and beyond. *Quantum*, 2:79.

Altaf Rahman and Vincent Ng. 2012. Resolving complex cases of definite pronouns: The winograd schema challenge. In *Proceedings of the 2012 Joint Conference on Empirical Methods in Natural Language Processing and Computational Natural Language Learning*, pages 777–789, Jeju Island, Korea. Association for Computational Linguistics.

Nils Reimers and Iryna Gurevych. 2019. Sentence-bert: Sentence embeddings using siamese bert-networks.

Fariska Z. Ruskanda, Muhammad Rifat Abiwardani, Muhammad Akram Al Bari, Kinantan Arya Bagaspati, Rahmat Mulyawan, Infall Syafalni, and Harashta Tatimma Larasati. 2022. Quantum representation for sentiment classification. In *2022 IEEE International Conference on Quantum Computing and Engineering (QCE)*, pages 67–78.

M. Sadrzadeh, S. Clark, and B. Coecke. 2013. The frobenius anatomy of word meanings i: subject and object relative pronouns. *Journal of Logic and Computation*, 23(6):1293–1317.

Mehrnoosh Sadrzadeh, Stephen Clark, and Bob Coecke. 2014. The frobenius anatomy of word meanings II: possessive relative pronouns. *Journal of Logic and Computation*, 26(2):785–815.

Dan Shepherd and Michael J. Bremner. 2009. Temporally unstructured quantum computation. *Proceedings of the Royal Society A: Mathematical, Physical and Engineering Sciences*, (2105):1413–1439.

J.C. Spall. 1998. Implementation of the simultaneous perturbation algorithm for stochastic optimization. *IEEE Transactions on Aerospace and Electronic Systems*, 34(3):817–823.

Mark Steedman. 2001. *The Syntactic Process*. The MIT Press.

Jonas Stein, Ivo Christ, Nicolas Kraus, Maximilian Balthasar Mansky, Robert Müller, and Claudia Linnhoff-Popien. 2023. Applying qnlp to sentiment analysis in finance.

R.S. Sutor. 2019. *Dancing with Qubits: How Quantum Computing Works and how it Can Change the World*. Expert Insight. Packt Publishing.

Hugo Touvron, Thibaut Lavril, Gautier Izacard, Xavier Martinet, Marie-Anne Lachaux, Timothée Lacroix, Baptiste Rozière, Naman Goyal, Eric Hambro, Faisal Azhar, Aurelien Rodriguez, Armand Joulin, Edouard Grave, and Guillaume Lample. 2023. Llama: Open and efficient foundation language models.

Hadi Wazni, Kin Ian Lo, Lachlan McPheat, and Mehrnoosh Sadrzadeh. 2022. A quantum natural language processing approach to pronoun resolution.

Richie Yeung and Dimitri Kartsaklis. 2021. A ccg-based version of the discocat framework.

Appendix

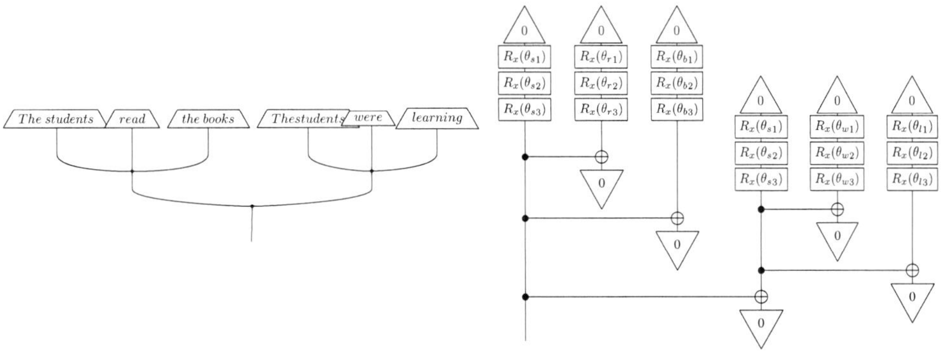

Figure 6: A Bag-of-Words diagram representing the discourse: *"The students read the books. They were learninig."* The diagram along with its transformation into a PQC.

- Template Example 1:
  - The sailors *{verb, phrasal verb, verb phrase}* the boats. They were *{adjective, gerund phrase}*
  - The *{adjective}* sailors *{verb, phrasal verb, verb phrase}* the boats. They were *{adjective, gerund phrase}*
  - The sailors *{verb, phrasal verb, verb phrase}* the *{adjective}* boats. They were *{adjective, gerund phrase}*
  - The *{adjective}* sailors *{verb, phrasal verb, verb phrase}* the *{adjective}* boats. They were *{adjective, gerund phrase}*
- Template Example 2:
  - The storm *{verb, verb phrase}* the flight. It was *{gerund phrase}*
  - The *{adjective}* storm *{verb, verb phrase}* the flight. It was *{gerund phrase}*
  - The storm *{verb, verb phrase}* the *{adjective}* flight. It was *{gerund phrase}*
  - The *{adjective}* storm *{verb, verb phrase}* the *{adjective}* flight. It was *{gerund phrase}*
- 8 distinct structural patterns for Template Example 2:
  - The storm *{verb, verb phrase}* the flight. It was *{gerund phrase (storm)}*.
  - The storm *{verb, verb phrase}* the flight. It was *{gerund phrase (flight)}*.
  - The *{adjective (storm)}* storm *{verb, verb phrase}* the flight. It was *{gerund phrase (storm)}*.
  - The *{adjective (storm)}* storm *{verb, verb phrase}* the flight. It was *{gerund phrase (flight)}*.
  - The storm *{verb, verb phrase}* the *{adjective (flight)}* flight. It was *{gerund phrase (flight)}*.
  - The storm *{verb, verb phrase}* the *{adjective (flight)}* flight. It was *{gerund phrase (storm)}*.
  - The *{adjective (storm)}* storm *{verb, verb phrase}* the *{adjective (flight)}* flight. It was *{gerund phrase (storm)}*.
  - The *{adjective (storm)}* storm *{verb, verb phrase}* the *{adjective (flight)}* flight. It was *{gerund phrase (flight)}*.

Scalar Anaphora: Annotating Degrees of Coreference in Text

Bingyang Ye and **Jingxuan Tu** and **Kyeongmin Rim** and **James Pustejovsky**
Department of Computer Science
Brandeis University
Waltham, Massachusetts
{byye,jxtu,krim,jamesp}@brandeis.edu

Abstract

In this paper, we examine the concept of coreference in natural language text, and the challenge of identifying when two or more narrative entities should be resolved as anaphorically bound, and hence viewed as semantically identical or related. To help answer this question, we propose a coreference scale (*Scalar Anaphora*) for determining the degree of similarity between an anaphoric expression and its antecedent in narratives. We create a corpus of pairs of such anaphors and antecedents and annotate the relations between them based on the newly defined scale. Our data shows that the ratio of human annotators' agreement score aligns with the scale of coreference. We also present the baseline results of predicting the scales using recent T5 and GPT-4 models, which suggests that predicting such fine-grained scales is still a challenging task for large language models. We will make the code and the data publicly available.

1 Introduction

Anaphora resolution involves identifying the mentions that contain anaphoric or coreferential relations and predicting the correct relation for the extracted mentions. Conventional anaphora resolution corpora such as OntoNotes (Marcus et al., 2011) and ACE (Doddington et al., 2004) focus largely on coreference. However, there are many "anaphora-related" phenomena that are extremely important for facilitating deeper linguistic analysis and modeling by modern NLP systems.

Bridging (Clark, 1975; Asher and Lascarides, 1998; Hawkins, 2015) is one such phenomena. It refers to a set of non-identity anaphoric relations. Despite the recent growing attention on bridging, existing corpora and methods (Uryupina et al., 2020; Yu et al., 2022) still treat the bridging resolution and coreference resolution as two independent problems, overlooking the linguistic closeness between anaphoric phenomena and coreferential identity, which leads to discrepancies of annotations on the same mention across corpora (Recasens et al., 2010).

To alleviate the principal complexity resulting from using a binary distinction of identity and non-identity, Recasens et al. (2011) proposed the concept of "Near-Identity" which denotes partial identity relations between mentions. Many previous works acknowledged the importance of having a mid-ground as Near-Identity (Uryupina et al., 2020; Rösiger et al., 2018), but did not include it in their annotation schema or modeling implementation for fear of introducing too much uncertainty. Recasens et al. (2012) is the first attempt to create a public corpus of near-identity. However, the whole typology of near-identity was treated as a coarsed weak and strong classifications, still leaving some gaps between identity, near-identity, bridging and non identity.

In this paper, we extend the themes from Recasens et al. (2010) and treat anaphora resolution as a continuum with a middle zone of near-identity relations. To supplement and enrich the notion of near-identity, we introduce *Scalar Anaphora*, a typology that categorizes near-identity with a simplified but more operationalized granularity, while unifying it with other anaphoric relations. Furthermore, we leverage the disagreements in the raw annotation of Phrase Detectives (PD) 3.0 (Yu et al., 2023) to create a dataset using Scalar Anaphora (SA) as the annotation schema. The presence of disagreement underscores the absence of a singular, unequivocal interpretation within a specific context for anaphora resolution, consistent with the concept of SA.

The major contributions outlined in this paper include:

- The introduction of *Scalar Anaphora*, a unified typology for anaphoric relations. Specifically, we define relations of *Coreference under Description* and *Coreference under Trans-*

Proceedings of the Sixth Workshop on Computational Models of Reference, Anaphora and Coreference (CRAC 2023), pages 28–38
December 6–7, 2023

formation to fill the gap between identity and non-identity while considering their semantic closeness on the scale of identity.

- We leverage the raw annotations in PD 3.0 release (Yu et al., 2023) to facilitate the detection of mentions with ambiguous anaphoric relation, and create a dataset of SA relations using our typology.
- We experiment with T5 and GPT-4 as baseline models for the evaluation of our anaphoric relations against human annotations. The results suggest that identifying ambiguous anaphoric relations in SA is still challenging.

2 Related Work

Anaphora resolution refers to the task of detecting the relation that holds between two textual entities in a text. Conventional linguistic anaphora designates coreference, where the two mentions refer to (denote) the same entity or concept. The Computational Linguistics literature has broadened this term to also allow for more general anaphoric relations, where the two mentions refer to different entities, but are linked via semantic, lexical, or encyclopedic relations (Hou et al., 2018). Most existing anaphora corpora only annotate coreference (Marcus et al., 2011; Yu et al., 2023). Within the wider definition of anaphora, however, the other major phenomenon of interest is bridging.

The Vieira / Poesio corpus (Poesio and Vieira, 1997) and GNOME (Poesio, 2004) are the two early attempts to annotate bridging. Since the release of the ARRAU corpus, more efforts have been dedicated to annotating bridging relations (Markert et al., 2012; Grishina, 2016; Rösiger, 2016; Zeldes, 2017; Rösiger et al., 2018). The Prague Dependency Treebank (Hajič et al., 2020) and the Polish Coreference Corpus (Ogrodniczuk et al., 2016) are other corpora annotating bridging in languages other than English. Due to the difficulty of detecting bridging (Poesio and Vieira, 1997; Vieira, 1998), most bridging corpora are still very small. Only ARRAU has a comparatively large annotations of bridging in English with 5,512 pairs of anaphor and antecedents. Moreover, these corpora all have rather diverse definitions and annotations of bridging which makes it even more difficult to do cross-corpus analysis and modeling (Rösiger et al., 2018).

Prior research on bridging resolution typically adopts two approaches: 1) incorporating bridging recognition within information status classification (Markert et al., 2012; Hou et al., 2013a); 2) focusing solely on antecedent selection, assuming prior completion of bridging recognition (Poesio et al., 2004; Hou et al., 2013b; Hou, 2018). Vieira and Poesio (2000) and Hou et al. (2014) also experimented with rule-based systems. More recently, there are a growing number of works using neural networks to tackle the problem (Yu and Poesio, 2020; Kantor and Globerson, 2019). Kantor and Globerson (2019) proposed the first neural model for full bridging resolution, leveraging a span-based neural model originally developed for entity coreference resolution. Hou (2020) proposed a neural approach to bridging resolution based on question answering.

Near-identity is also an anaphoric phenomenon that bears great linguistic values. The near-identity relations are akin to "bridging anaphora" as indirect connections requiring inference, yet distinct as they cannot be considered anything other than identity (Recasens et al., 2010). Since Recasens et al. (2011) introduced the concept of Near-Identity and proposed to redefine coreference as a scalar relation, a series of works on near-identity have been made. Recasens et al. (2010) proposed a typology of near-identity relations that comprised fifteen relations under five families. Preliminary annotation were also made to prove that the inter-annotator agreement is stable enough for a more extensive annotation of near-identity (Recasens et al., 2012) on NP4E corpus (Hasler et al., 2006). The granularity of typology in Recasens et al. (2010), however, was lost in the annotation as all the relations were labeled as either weak or strong near-identity. Ogrodniczuk et al. (2016) also contains near-identity relations in the corpus. These works, despite providing a strong theoretical base for research in near-identity, still lack empirical modeling and evaluation. Our paper presents a typology of anaphoric relations by merging and simplifying the typology of near-identity in Recasens et al. (2010). The Scalar Anaphora typology offers a means to establish a corpus with more nuanced subtypes of anaphoric relations, organized semantically in a hierarchical manner, as these SA relations correspond to varying degrees of identity on a scale. Additionally, our study delves into the modeling of SA relations and assesses their alignment with human annotations to explore the practicality of this schema.

Recasens et al. (2010) defined the anaphoric relation between one facet or attribute of an entity and the entity itself as a subtype of near-identity. It is also referred as metonymy in Markert and Nissim (2007) and Pustejovsky and Rumshisky (2009). In this work, we are only treating metonymy as a part of the near-identity. The type structure proposed in Generative Lexicon theory (Pustejovsky, 1995) could serve as the theoretical approach to further address the categorization of dot objects (systematic polysemies).

Recent work also studied the tracking of transformation or changes of entities within the frame of anaphora resolution. Fang et al. (2022) and Rim et al. (2023) annotated anaphoric relations including coreference and bridging for procedural texts. They treat the transformation of entities, e.g., *oil* mixed with *salt* being later referred to as a *mixture*, as a bridging relation. Rim et al. (2023) also defined the concept of Coreference under Transformation, which is the first attempt to introduce transformation of events into the scope of anaphora resolution. Oguz et al. (2022) presented a multimodal anaphora corpus on recipes where the transformation is annotated as a near-identity rather than bridging. Zeldes (2021) also argued the importance of tracking the change of entities over time for coreference resolution problem and proposed adding a new layer of annotation on "scope" for OntoNotes.

Learning from disagreements among coders has been a growing topic in the NLP field. An emerging trend in dataset creation involves moving beyond a solitary "gold" annotation to encompass the inclusion of the entirety of raw annotations provided by coders.Uma et al. (2021) and Leonardelli et al. (2023) posted shared tasks to model the disagreements among annotators in a variety of fields including coreference resolution, pos tagging, humour detection, etc. Recasens et al. (2012) also created the NIDENT corpus by automatically identifying near-identity relations using human coders' disagreements.

3 Defining Scalar Anaphora

For this paper, we propose a coreference scale called Scalar Anaphora, for determining the degree of similarity between an anaphoric expression and its antecedent in narratives. Figure 1 shows the typology of Scalar Anaphora as a decision tree, where neighboring nodes are semantically closer on the scale of identity. Following Recasens et al. (2010), we believe anaphoric binding relations in text are best viewed as expressing degrees of identity between the entities. In this paper, we go further and argue that these types can be partially ordered on a scale of referential similarity.

Formally, for two *narrtive entities*, e_1 and e_2, we identify five anaphoric relations on the scale based on the semantic closeness between them. The scale begins by distinguishing between the relation of (strict) *Identity* and (strict) *Non-identity*. If e_1 and e_2 are substitutible under both transparent and opaque contexts, then we say e_1 and e_2 are coreferential or Identical. For example, conventional coreference clusters, e.g., including *Clinton*, *Hillary Clinton*, and *she*, illustrate semantic substitutibility between all members of the cluster, including opaque contexts. Hence, in a belief context, such as *believes x is a good Senator*, any member of the cluster can be substituted without changing the truth value. Strict identity is the strongest relation of similarity.

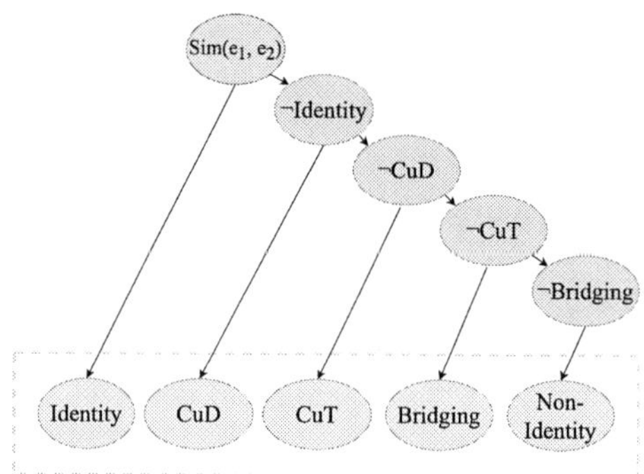

Figure 1: Typology of Scalar Anaphora.

The nearest relation to this comes about by identifying when a pair of entities is not substitutible under both opaque contexts and non-opaque. This arises with occupational and functional descriptions of entities, complicating substitutions.

(1) **Clinton**[ANTECEDENT], **the Senator**[ANAPHOR] from New York, voiced her concerns about the proposed bill during the congressional hearing.

For example, in 1, while the pair ("Clinton", "the Senator") are substitutible under non-opaque contexts (being female, American, medium height), the functional nominal *senator* can be embedded in an opaque context ("a very good senator"), while not allowing Clinton to necessarily be judged as good. Hence, we introduce a class of *Coreference under Description (CuD)* to describe the semantic relation between two entities, if they are substitutible only under non-opaque contexts. Hence, *CuD* is weaker than *Identity*.

The next class on the scale of similarity is defined by *Coreference under Transformation (CuT)*. This includes entities that are "substance identical", but are not formally identical. For entities that undergo changes by virtue of explicitly mentioned actions or processes (slicing, chopping, grilling), If two entities denote identical substances, regardless of individuation (form), we say they are substance identical. If the formal difference is the result of a transformative action, e.g., chopping or grilling, we say e_1 and e_2 are coreferential under transformation, e.g., *an onion* and *the chopped onion*. As a result, *CuT* is weaker than *CuD*.

The final distinction is defined by identifying whether the two entities are conceptually of the same type or different type. This of course includes Clark's original examples of *bridging* relations, where we focus on tangible relations such as part-of, member-of and location. Clearly, *Bridging* is weaker than *CuT*. If none of these relations holds, we identify two entities as being in a strictly non-coreferential relation. The extremum of dissimilarity, *Non-Identity*, is therefore weaker than *Bridging*.

4 Corpus Annotation

Inspired by the method in Recasens et al. (2012) of automatically extracting mentions of near-identity relations by leveraging coders' disagreement, we seek to use disagreement scores to speed up the process of identifying mention pairs with anaphoric relations rather than annotating exhaustively. Once the pairs are automatically extracted, we apply our schema of SA to them and annotate the scale of annaphora for each of the relation they hold.

4.1 Data Preparation

PD 3.0 (Yu et al., 2023) is a corpus collecting multiple human judgments about anaphoric reference crowdsourced in the form of Games-With-A-Purpose (Von Ahn, 2006) on fictions and Wikipedia texts. During annotation, players either aim at labeling antecedent for a given anaphor or they make a binary anaphoric judgment about other player's annotation where the participants have to agree or disagree with the interpretation. We prepare the annotation by extracting mentions from the PD 3.0 corpus because of its rich annotations. Every mention in the texts is at least annotated by 8 players (20 in average). And for each different anaphoric judgment of two mentions, there are at least 4 players conducting the validation. The disagreement among the players for each pair is also reported.

We only use 35 Wikipedia texts from the PD 3.0 corpus gold data as our source data because comparing to fictions, Wikipedia tends to contain more proper nouns and less pronouns, which usually hold identity relation with their antecedents. The other reason is that Wikipedia requires more common knowledge than interpretation of the context, which results in less confusion among the annotators.

We parse the raw data from masxml files and extract candidate anaphoric relation pairs. Each pair has two mentions *anaphor* and *antecedent*, along with an array of human judgments agreeing or disagreeing with this interpretation. We calculate the DISAGREEMENT SCORE (DS) by dividing the number of disagreements by the total number of judgments. The higher the DS, the higher the ratio of disagreement among annotators.

Intuitively we hypothesize that the DS could indicate the scale of identity between the *anaphor* and *antecedent*, and the DS will be inversely proportional to the identity scale, i.e., with the DS increasing, the two mentions are less identical. In that sense, we are binning our set of pairs into three bins according to their DS assuming that different bins would show corresponding distributions of SA relations. We set the three bins as [0, 0.4], [0.4, 0.7] and [0.7, 1.0].

While there are 2,939 pairs extracted from the PD corpus, we do not have enough resources to annotate every one of them. To keep the topic diversity from the Wikipedia texts, for the document from each topic, we randomly sample three pairs from each DS bin. After careful examination, we exclude 7 cases where the sentence contexts are limited or missing for determining the anaphoric relation of the pair. Finally we have 308 pairs that are split into three batches.

4.2 Scalar Anaphora Annotation

Given a pair of *anaphor* and *antecedent*, and their sentence contexts, we ask annotators to annotate the pairwise anaphoric relation. After each round of annotation, annotators would adjudicate disagreements and create the harmonized annotation. All 308 pairs are dually annotated in three batches by two expert annotators from the linguistics and computer science departments of a US-based university. The annotation involves each annotator classifying the relation into the SA typology by judging the degree of identity between pairs of mentions. We design the annotation workflow based on the SA typology from Figure 1 and follow its decision-tree based methodology:

1. The annotator should first judge if the two mentions are strictly identical, which means they appear to denote the same individual. If yes, annotate IDENTITY.
2. If not, then check if one mention represents one facet or some attributes other than formal role of the other mention. For example, a company produces a product (i.e., a dot object with a metonymic interpretation (Pustejovsky, 1995)). If yes, annotate CUD.
3. Then check if one mention is substance identical to the other mention after some transformative actions where they are no longer strictly identical but still share some common characteristics. If yes, then annotate CUT.
4. Next, check if both mentions point to two entities that are conceptually of the same type or different type, while holding some relations such as part-of or location. If yes, then annotate BRIDGING.
5. Finally, if none of that above relations holds and the two mentions point to different entities, annotate NON-IDENTITY.

We use pairwise F1 and Cohen's Kappa as our metrics for Inter-Annotator Agreement (IAA). Table 1 shows the IAA from each round of the annotation. The complexity of annotating CuD and BRIDGING leads to most of the disagreement from the first round of the annotation. However, as annotators are getting more familiar with the SA typology, the IAA increases and reaches the highest in the last round.

The IAA for each relation in F1 is shown in Table 2. CUD, CUT and NON-IDENTITY constitute the relations with the highest disagreement in that they are of fewer instances and they tend to be more confusing because of their inherit ambiguity. For example, CUD are often mistaken as BRIDGING where the attribute of an entity is regarded as a relation:

	$F1$	Cohen's κ
Round 1	51.43	0.31
Round 2	66.67	0.51
Round 3	76.19	0.64

Table 1: IAA of each annotation round.

(2) **Laramie cigarettes** [ANTECEDENT], seeing an opportunity to sell **their products** [ANAPHOR] to children legally, offers to buy the rights to market tomacco for $150 million.

For CUT, the nature of narration in Wikipedia data exerts more subtlety onto the transformation unlike procedural texts. In 3, *Henry* undergoes a series of events including captivity and location change. However, one annotator overlooked the transformation and labeled CUT as IDENTITY.

(3) a. **Henry** [ANTECEDENT] was found off the coast of North Wales in a lobster pot, and is in captivity at the Blackpool Sea Life Centre in North West England;
b. **Henry** [ANAPHOR] is going to be in a new exhibit with an octopus at the Blackpool Sea Life Centre, entitled "Suckers".

The reason why the disagreement for NON-IDENTITY is low is that judgment is heavily context based. The anaphor and antecedent are usually similar strings but actually refer to two different entities after contextualization.

(4) An advantage of the knork is that it can be used easily by people who have **only one arm** [ANTECEDENT]; Roald Dahl reports in Boy how his father invented a knork precursor as a result of losing **his arm** [ANAPHOR].

We are pleased to report a high level of agreement in the annotation of both IDENTITY and BRIDGING instances. The robust concordance observed in IDENTITY annotations can be attributed to their relatively straightforward criteria, primarily involving exact string matching and explicit pronoun references. In the case of BRIDGING, the flexibility of its annotation criteria facilitates the discernment of tangible relations between mentions.

In our final corpus (Table 2), the ratio of near-identity (57.79%) in all annotations of anaphora is significantly higher than 12%-16% which is reported in (Recasens et al., 2012) as we have a more strict definition of NON-IDENTITY and a broader definition of BRIDGING resulting in a shift from NON-IDENTITY to BRIDGING.

	Count	Ratio (%)	IAA (F1)
IDENTITY	114	37.0	75.98
CUD	31	10.1	40.68
CUT	18	5.8	37.04
BRIDGING	129	41.9	70.87
NON-IDENTITY	16	5.2	36.36
OVERALL	308	100	65.31

Table 2: Statistics of annotation in terms of SA relation.

4.3 Correlation between Scales and Disagreement

To further understand whether the disagreement of the mention pairs from the PD 3.0 corpus can help identify high-quality candidates for our annotation, we investigate the possible correlations between the SA relation types and the DS of the mention pairs. We start by calculating the Spearman Rank Correlation coefficient (Spearman, 1961) between SA and DS. The score is 0.2248 which indicates there is a modest correlation between the two variables. Figure 2 details the distribution of SA relations when grouping them into the bins that are used in our annotation. IDENTITY is the relation with the highest proportion, showing that it is less confusing. The proportions of CuD and CuT remain similar across bins of low and medium DS and decrease in the high DS bin. This indicates that the two relations tend to trigger low and medium disagreements among annotators and behave like IDENTITY. Most NON-IDENTITY cases are in the final bin, indicating that it is the most confusing among all relations. BRIDGING, being the most dominant relation in the medium and high DS bins, has a similar trend of appearing more in the bins of higher DS as NON-IDENTITY.

Table 3 shows the average DS of each relation. The DS of IDENTITY is lower while the other relations all demonstrate a comparatively high DS. Notably, the average DS increases as the relation becomes more towards non-identity on the anaphoric scale, which aligns with our hypothesis that DS could be inversely proportionate to identity. Overall, we believe that the DS is a useful resource for anaphoric relation annotation, and the correlation could be more statistically significant with more annotations.

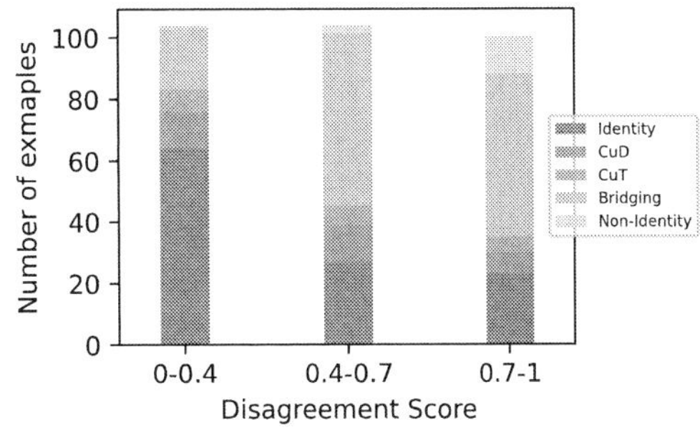

Figure 2: Distribution of SA relation in different DS bins (left inclusive).

	Average DS
IDENTITY	0.376
CUD	0.465
CUT	0.477
BRIDGING	0.594
NON-IDENTITY	0.727

Table 3: Average DS of each relation.

5 Scalar Anaphora Resolution

In this section, we present experiments of the task for anaphora resolution with fine-grained relations that we defined in the SA. We explore baselines from language models and provide further insights on our data. In our experiments, we formalize SA resolutions the task of identifying the SA relation between each mention pair given the sentence context of the entity.[1]

5.1 Data Processing

We use our annotated data for model training and evaluation. For all the pairs from each SA relations, we randomly sample 80% of the pairs for training and hold out the other 20% for testing. Table 4 shows the train test split for the experiments. Since some relation have much fewer pairs than the others, sampling by relation type is useful for ensuring the data balance between train and test.

Since PD only contains human-selected pairs where the two entities have associations, there is no "real" non-identity relation between the existing pairs. With that in mind, for each Wikipedia topic,

[1]Unlike conventional coreference resolution tasks, we provide gold mentions and only predict the relations between the mentions as our baselines are designed for providing insights on the new relations from SA.

we generate two negative pairs with mentions randomly sampled from all the mentions from this topic. Those negative pairs will also be labeled as NON-IDENTITY in modeling. When reporting the results, we will label these pairs as NEGATIVE.

	Train	Test
IDENTITY	91	23
CUD	25	6
CUT	14	4
BRIDGING	103	26
NON-IDENTITY	13	3
NEGATIVE	56	14
OVERALL	302	76

Table 4: Train test split of the SA dataset.

5.2 Experiment 1: Scalar Anaphora with T5

Experiment Setup We use the recent sequence-to-sequence generation model T5 (Raffel et al., 2020) as the baseline. We set the input sequence as the question answering format with entities that are highlighted in the text. An example sequence is shown in Figure 3. The input includes the questions and the context where the mentions are wrapped by a pair of squared brackets ([...]).The output is the SA relation. We fine-tune the T5-base model on the training set, and evaluate the results on the testing set. Model performance was evaluated using precision, recall and F1-score.

Input text:
queston: What is the relation between [mainly wealthier nations] and [these countries]?
context: VHEMT spreads its message ... reaching [mainly wealthier nations] .
A few of [these countries] already have fertility rates below ...
output text:
Bridging

Figure 3: Example of T5 model input and output for SA resolution task.

Results Table 5 shows the results of the pairwise SA relation classification on our test set. IDENTITY and BRIDGING are the two relations that achieve relatively high F1 scores. The reasons are: 1. There are more training examples; 2. The two relations are relatively easy to categorize which aligns with human annotation. The result of randomly picked negative examples is also relatively high in that they are mostly just completely distinct entities thus also straightforward to distinguish. It is not surprising to see that the performance on CUD is low. T5 often times confuse it with IDENTITY. The model also fail to predict any CUT or NON-IDENTITY relation. Besides the fewer number of examples, the ambiguity of the two relations also contributes to the poor performance. Notably, T5 labels all examples of these two relations as IDENTITY.

(5) It bought this land as **a standard-sized lot in 1903** [ANTECEDENT], but the City widened Pender Street in 1912 and expropriated 24 feet (7.3 m) of **the lot** [ANAPHOR].

(6) **The bulb** [ANTECEDENT] was officially listed in the Guinness Book of World Records as "the Most Durable Light", in 1972, replacing **another bulb** [ANAPHOR] in Fort Worth, Texas.

For example, in 5, the relation of CUT is mistakenly predicted as IDENTITY. This indicates that T5 model is unable to capture the transformative event the antecedent undergoes; while in 6 the model also failed to detect that *the bulb* and *another bulb* are distinct entities in a complicated context.

	P	R	F1
IDENTITY	56.25	78.26	65.45
CUD	100	16.67	28.57
CUT	0	0	0
BRIDGING	60.00	57.69	58.82
NON-IDENTITY	0	0	0
NEGATIVE	100	28.57	44.44
OVERALL	52.71	30.20	32.88

Table 5: Pairwise relation classification results on the test set with T5.

5.3 Experiment 2: Scalar Anaphora with GPT-4

Experiment Setup We experiment with GPT-4 (Brown et al., 2020; OpenAI, 2023) as another baseline for the SA resolution task. Comparing to the T5 baseline with fully supervised learning (§5.2), we use GPT-4 with few-shot prompt learning. In each prompt, we use a single set of 5 exemplars from the training set and a human-created instruction on how to perform the task. We conduct prompt tuning on a small subset of the training set, and evaluate the best prompt on the testing test. Similar to T5 baseline, Model performance was evaluated using precision, recall and F1-score.

Prompt Tuning We randomly sample 25 pairs from the training set as the "seeds" to evaluate the GPT-4 performance with different prompt formulations. Table 6 shows the prompt combinations

```
The following describes the task that predicts the relation between two phrases from the text.
The text spans of the phrase are wrapped within "[]". In this task, we define 5 types of relations:
    - Non-Identity: The two phrases point to different entities
    - Identity: The two phrases point to the same entity.  They have the same set of attributes,
                or one phrase represents the most important feature of the other phrase.
    - Role: One phrase represents one facet or some attributes of the other phrase. But this attribute should not be the most important one.
            For example, a company produces a product, is headquartered in a location, has a president, etc.
    - Transformation: Entity from one phrase undergo some transformation of which the outcome is no longer
    - Bridging: Both phrases point to two different entities, but these two entities usually related in a way that is not explicitly stated
```

```
The following describes the task that predicts the relation between two phrases from the text.
The text spans of the phrase are wrapped within "[]".
Please predicts the relation in the following order:
    1. Both phrases point to two different entities, but these two entities often holds some relations. E.g., one phrase refers to something
       that is part of the other phrase or one phrase could cause the other phrase to happen. Please predict Bridging.
    2. If both phrases point to two different entities and is not Bridging, see if one phrase represents one facet or
       some attributes of the other phrase. For example, a company produces a product, is headquartered in a location, etc. Please predict Role
    3. If both phrases point to two different entities and is not Bridging nor Role, please predict Non-Identity.
    4. If the two phrases point to the same entities, check if the entity from on phrase undergo any transformation or event.
       If so, please predict Transformation.
    5. If the two phrases point to the same entities, and it is not Transformation. Then please predict Identity.
```

Figure 4: Flat instruction (top) and hierarchical instruction (bottom) part of the prompt.

in the experiments. Each type of the prompt consists of an instruction and 5 exemplars (5-shot). *0-shot* only contains the instruction. *5-shot-random* contains random human-generated exemplars; *5-shot-domain* contains in-domain exemplars from the training set; *5-shot-CoT* adds additional chain of thought (Wei et al., 2022) to each in-domain exemplar. We generate two types of instructions for the prompts (Figure 4). The flat one instructs the model to predict the relations all as separate and individual classes, while the hierarchy one instructs the model to make decisions following several temporally ordered steps.

	Flat Instruct.	Hierarchical Instruct.
0-shot	✔	✔
5-shot-random	✔	✔
5-shot-domain	✔	✔
5-shot-CoT	✔	✔

Table 6: GPT-4 prompt combinations for the SA resolution baseline.

Table 7 shows the results on the 25 pairs using different prompts. We achieve the highest macro F1 score with few-shot tuning using CoT and Hierarchical instructions. For the following experiments with GPT-4, we will continue using this prompt setting.

Results Table 8 shows the results of GPT-4 using few-shot learning with CoT and hierarchical structure. The model achieves pretty good results on IDENTITY and CUT. However, the performances of the other relations are not very high.

Comparing the results of GPT-4 in table 8 with that of T5, we can notice that the overall performance slightly decreases as well as the performance for most individual relation. This is likely due to supervised learning outperforming few-shot learning since the task is non-trivial and it is naturally difficult to fully understand all the relations with just a few examples. The performance of relation IDENTITY is consistently high across the two models, while NON-IDENTITY still cannot be correctly predicted. This complies with our assumptions that IDENTITY relation is fairly easy to categorize and NON-IDENTITY is very confusing. We are glad to see that the F1 score of CUT increases significantly after explicitly asking the model to pay more attention to the transformative event. However, it is disappointing to see that the performances on CUD, BRIDGING and NEGATIVE all drop.

		P	R	F1
Flat	0-shot	32.41	**40.00**	33.63
	5-shot-random	36.94	33.33	26.79
	5-shot-domain	20.50	30.00	21.30
	5-shot-CoT	40.00	**40.00**	36.41
Hierarchy	0-shot	44.44	30.00	34.78
	5-shot-random	46.30	30.00	27.78
	5-shot-domain	41.32	30.00	34.76
	5-shot-CoT	**50.11**	36.67	**37.90**

Table 7: Pairwise relation classification results on 25 random examples with different prompt settings.

	P	R	F1
IDENTITY	46.81	95.65	62.86
CUD	10.00	16.67	12.50
CUT	40.00	50.00	44.44
BRIDGING	66.67	15.38	25.00
NON-IDENTITY	0	0	0
NEGATIVE	100	14.29	25.00
OVERALL	43.91	32.00	28.30

Table 8: Pairwise relation classification results on the test set with GPT-4.

6 Conclusion

We have proposed the Scalar Anaphora, a unified typology for anaphoric relations that can be identified and evaluated between coreference and non-coreference by considering their semantic closeness on the scale of identity. To that end, we have defined *Coreference under Description* and *Coreference under Transformation*, two additional granular relations that express difference semantic closeness on the scale of identity. We have constructed a new dataset that encodes manually annotated anaphoric relation between each mention pair, and our annotations have been able to show that the anaphoric relation correlates with human judgments on the closeness of each mention pair on the identity scale. We have also performed pairwise classification tasks on the anaphoric relations and presented baselines from recent T5 and GPT-4 models. The results have shown that the understanding of anaphoric relations remains challenging to current large language models. In future research, we intend to apply our method and annotation to more data and a broader range of text genres. We will also explore the validity and application of the anaphoric scale typology on the chain of cluster of entities and mentions by not limiting it to pairwise evaluation.

Ethics Statement

In conducting this research and preparing this paper, we want to affirm that our research has solely focused on scientific inquiry and there are no ethical concerns or issues that have arisen in the course of our study.

Limitations

Since the goal of PD annotation is to only annotate coreference, the raw data we process would be biased towards identity, and many cases of other SA relations could be omitted. And during data preparation stage, we exclude the human expert annotations and only focus on crowdsourced annotations in PD. In future work, we plan to take advantage of the expert annotations in determining the DS since it is of higher quality. Also due to the nature of narrative texts, the number of instances of CuT is low. A better understanding of how transformation affects the semantic closeness of an entity to its antecedent requires an extended annotation on procedural texts where tranformative events are more prevalent. To address the aforementioned issues, a new corpus of annotation of SA relations on different types of texts is needed.

References

Nicholas Asher and Alex Lascarides. 1998. Bridging. *Journal of Semantics*, 15(1):83–113.

Tom B. Brown, Benjamin Mann, Nick Ryder, Melanie Subbiah, Jared Kaplan, Prafulla Dhariwal, Arvind Neelakantan, Pranav Shyam, Girish Sastry, Amanda Askell, Sandhini Agarwal, Ariel Herbert-Voss, Gretchen Krueger, T. J. Henighan, Rewon Child, Aditya Ramesh, Daniel M. Ziegler, Jeff Wu, Clemens Winter, Christopher Hesse, Mark Chen, Eric Sigler, Mateusz Litwin, Scott Gray, Benjamin Chess, Jack Clark, Christopher Berner, Sam McCandlish, Alec Radford, Ilya Sutskever, and Dario Amodei. 2020. Language models are few-shot learners. *ArXiv*, abs/2005.14165.

Herbert H. Clark. 1975. Bridging. In *Theoretical Issues in Natural Language Processing*.

George R Doddington, Alexis Mitchell, Mark A Przybocki, Lance A Ramshaw, Stephanie M Strassel, and Ralph M Weischedel. 2004. The automatic content extraction (ace) program-tasks, data, and evaluation. In *Lrec*, volume 2, pages 837–840. Lisbon.

Biaoyan Fang, Timothy Baldwin, and Karin Verspoor. 2022. What does it take to bake a cake? the RecipeRef corpus and anaphora resolution in procedural text. In *Findings of the Association for Computational Linguistics: ACL 2022*, pages 3481–3495, Dublin, Ireland. Association for Computational Linguistics.

Yulia Grishina. 2016. Experiments on bridging across languages and genres. In *Proceedings of the Workshop on Coreference Resolution Beyond OntoNotes (CORBON 2016)*, pages 7–15.

Jan Hajič, Eduard Bejček, Jaroslava Hlavacova, Marie Mikulová, Milan Straka, Jan Štěpánek, and Barbora Štěpánková. 2020. Prague dependency treebank - consolidated 1.0. In *Proceedings of the Twelfth Language Resources and Evaluation Conference*, pages 5208–5218, Marseille, France. European Language Resources Association.

Laura Hasler, Constantin Orasan, and Karin Naumann. 2006. NPs for events: Experiments in coreference annotation. In *Proceedings of the Fifth International Conference on Language Resources and Evaluation (LREC'06)*, Genoa, Italy. European Language Resources Association (ELRA).

John Hawkins. 2015. *Definiteness and indefiniteness: A study in reference and grammaticality prediction.* Routledge.

Yufang Hou. 2018. A deterministic algorithm for bridging anaphora resolution. In *Proceedings of the 2018 Conference on Empirical Methods in Natural Language Processing*, pages 1938–1948, Brussels, Belgium. Association for Computational Linguistics.

Yufang Hou. 2020. Bridging anaphora resolution as question answering. In *Proceedings of the 58th Annual Meeting of the Association for Computational Linguistics*, pages 1428–1438, Online. Association for Computational Linguistics.

Yufang Hou, Katja Markert, and Michael Strube. 2013a. Cascading collective classification for bridging anaphora recognition using a rich linguistic feature set. In *Proceedings of the 2013 Conference on Empirical Methods in Natural Language Processing*, pages 814–820.

Yufang Hou, Katja Markert, and Michael Strube. 2013b. Global inference for bridging anaphora resolution. In *Proceedings of the 2013 Conference of the North American Chapter of the Association for Computational Linguistics: Human Language Technologies*, pages 907–917, Atlanta, Georgia. Association for Computational Linguistics.

Yufang Hou, Katja Markert, and Michael Strube. 2014. A rule-based system for unrestricted bridging resolution: Recognizing bridging anaphora and finding links to antecedents. In *Proceedings of the 2014 Conference on Empirical Methods in Natural Language Processing (EMNLP)*, pages 2082–2093, Doha, Qatar. Association for Computational Linguistics.

Yufang Hou, Katja Markert, and Michael Strube. 2018. Unrestricted bridging resolution. *Computational Linguistics*, 44(2):237–284.

Ben Kantor and Amir Globerson. 2019. Coreference resolution with entity equalization. In *Proceedings of the 57th Annual Meeting of the Association for Computational Linguistics*, pages 673–677, Florence, Italy. Association for Computational Linguistics.

Elisa Leonardelli, Gavin Abercrombie, Dina Almanea, Valerio Basile, Tommaso Fornaciari, Barbara Plank, Verena Rieser, Alexandra Uma, and Massimo Poesio. 2023. SemEval-2023 task 11: Learning with disagreements (LeWiDi). In *Proceedings of the 17th International Workshop on Semantic Evaluation (SemEval-2023)*, pages 2304–2318, Toronto, Canada. Association for Computational Linguistics.

RWEHM Marcus, Martha Palmer, RBSPL Ramshaw, and Nianwen Xue. 2011. Ontonotes: A large training corpus for enhanced processing. *Joseph Olive, Caitlin Christianson, andJohn McCary, editors, Handbook of Natural LanguageProcessing and Machine Translation: DARPA GlobalAutonomous Language Exploitation*.

Katja Markert, Yufang Hou, and Michael Strube. 2012. Collective classification for fine-grained information status. In *Proceedings of the 50th Annual Meeting of the Association for Computational Linguistics (Volume 1: Long Papers)*, pages 795–804.

Katja Markert and Malvina Nissim. 2007. SemEval-2007 task 08: Metonymy resolution at SemEval-2007. In *Proceedings of the Fourth International Workshop on Semantic Evaluations (SemEval-2007)*, pages 36–41, Prague, Czech Republic. Association for Computational Linguistics.

Maciej Ogrodniczuk, Katarzyna Głowińska, Mateusz Kopeć, Agata Savary, and Magdalena Zawisławska. 2016. Polish coreference corpus. In *Human Language Technology. Challenges for Computer Science and Linguistics: 6th Language and Technology Conference, LTC 2013, Poznań, Poland, December 7-9, 2013. Revised Selected Papers 6*, pages 215–226. Springer.

Cennet Oguz, Ivana Kruijff-Korbayova, Emmanuel Vincent, Pascal Denis, and Josef van Genabith. 2022. Chop and change: Anaphora resolution in instructional cooking videos. In *Findings of the Association for Computational Linguistics: AACL-IJCNLP 2022*, pages 364–374, Online only. Association for Computational Linguistics.

OpenAI. 2023. Gpt-4 technical report. *ArXiv*, abs/2303.08774.

M Poesio. 2004. The mate/gnome scheme for anaphoric annotation. In *Proceedings of SIGDIAL*, pages 168–175.

Massimo Poesio, Rahul Mehta, Axel Maroudas, and Janet Hitzeman. 2004. Learning to resolve bridging references. In *Proceedings of the 42nd Annual Meeting of the Association for Computational Linguistics (ACL-04)*, pages 143–150.

Massimo Poesio and Renata Vieira. 1997. A corpus-based investigation of definite description use. *arXiv preprint cmp-lg/9710007*.

James Pustejovsky. 1995. *The Generative Lexicon*. MIT Press, Cambridge, MA.

James Pustejovsky and Anna Rumshisky. 2009. SemEval-2010 task 7: Argument selection and coercion. In *Proceedings of the Workshop on Semantic Evaluations: Recent Achievements and Future Directions (SEW-2009)*, pages 88–93, Boulder, Colorado. Association for Computational Linguistics.

Colin Raffel, Noam Shazeer, Adam Roberts, Katherine Lee, Sharan Narang, Michael Matena, Yanqi Zhou, Wei Li, and Peter J. Liu. 2020. Exploring the limits of transfer learning with a unified text-to-text transformer. *Journal of Machine Learning Research*, 21(140):1–67.

Marta Recasens, Eduard Hovy, and M. Antònia Martí. 2010. A typology of near-identity relations for coreference (NIDENT). In *Proceedings of the Seventh International Conference on Language Resources and Evaluation (LREC'10)*, Valletta, Malta. European Language Resources Association (ELRA).

Marta Recasens, Eduard H. Hovy, and Maria Antònia Martí. 2011. Identity, non-identity, and near-identity: Addressing the complexity of coreference. *Lingua*, 121:1138–1152.

Marta Recasens, M. Antònia Martí, and Constantin Orasan. 2012. Annotating near-identity from coreference disagreements. In *Proceedings of the Eighth International Conference on Language Resources and Evaluation (LREC'12)*, pages 165–172, Istanbul, Turkey. European Language Resources Association (ELRA).

Kyeongmin Rim, Jingxuan Tu, Bingyang Ye, Marc Verhagen, Eben Holderness, and James Pustejovsky. 2023. The coreference under transformation labeling dataset: Entity tracking in procedural texts using event models. In *Findings of the Association for Computational Linguistics: ACL 2023*, pages 12448–12460, Toronto, Canada. Association for Computational Linguistics.

Ina Rösiger. 2016. Scicorp: A corpus of english scientific articles annotated for information status analysis. In *Proceedings of the Tenth International Conference on Language Resources and Evaluation (LREC'16)*, pages 1743–1749.

Ina Rösiger, Maximilian Köper, Kim Anh Nguyen, and Sabine Schulte im Walde. 2018. Integrating predictions from neural-network relation classifiers into coreference and bridging resolution. In *Proceedings of the First Workshop on Computational Models of Reference, Anaphora and Coreference*, pages 44–49.

Charles Spearman. 1961. The proof and measurement of association between two things.

Alexandra Uma, Tommaso Fornaciari, Anca Dumitrache, Tristan Miller, Jon Chamberlain, Barbara Plank, Edwin Simpson, and Massimo Poesio. 2021. SemEval-2021 task 12: Learning with disagreements. In *Proceedings of the 15th International Workshop on Semantic Evaluation (SemEval-2021)*, pages 338–347, Online. Association for Computational Linguistics.

Olga Uryupina, Ron Artstein, Antonella Bristot, Federica Cavicchio, Francesca Delogu, Kepa J Rodriguez, and Massimo Poesio. 2020. Annotating a broad range of anaphoric phenomena, in a variety of genres: the arrau corpus. *Natural Language Engineering*, 26(1):95–128.

Renata Vieira. 1998. Definite description resolution in unrestricted texts. *Unpublished doctoral dissertation. University of Edinburgh, Centre for Cognitive Science.*

Renata Vieira and Massimo Poesio. 2000. An empirically-based system for processing definite descriptions. *Computational Linguistics*, 26(4):539–593.

Luis Von Ahn. 2006. Games with a purpose. *Computer*, 39(6):92–94.

Jason Wei, Xuezhi Wang, Dale Schuurmans, Maarten Bosma, Ed Huai hsin Chi, F. Xia, Quoc Le, and Denny Zhou. 2022. Chain of thought prompting elicits reasoning in large language models. *ArXiv*, abs/2201.11903.

Juntao Yu, Sopan Khosla, Ramesh Manuvinakurike, Lori Levin, Vincent Ng, Massimo Poesio, Michael Strube, and Carolyn Rosé. 2022. The CODI-CRAC 2022 shared task on anaphora, bridging, and discourse deixis in dialogue. In *Proceedings of the CODI-CRAC 2022 Shared Task on Anaphora, Bridging, and Discourse Deixis in Dialogue*, pages 1–14, Gyeongju, Republic of Korea. Association for Computational Linguistics.

Juntao Yu, Silviu Paun, Maris Camilleri, Paloma Garcia, Jon Chamberlain, Udo Kruschwitz, and Massimo Poesio. 2023. Aggregating crowdsourced and automatic judgments to scale up a corpus of anaphoric reference for fiction and Wikipedia texts. In *Proceedings of the 17th Conference of the European Chapter of the Association for Computational Linguistics*, pages 767–781, Dubrovnik, Croatia. Association for Computational Linguistics.

Juntao Yu and Massimo Poesio. 2020. Multitask learning-based neural bridging reference resolution. In *Proceedings of the 28th International Conference on Computational Linguistics*, pages 3534–3546, Barcelona, Spain (Online). International Committee on Computational Linguistics.

Amir Zeldes. 2017. The gum corpus: Creating multilayer resources in the classroom. *Language Resources and Evaluation*, 51(3):581–612.

Amir Zeldes. 2021. Can we fix the scope for coreference? problems and solutions for benchmarks beyond ontonotes. *arXiv preprint arXiv:2112.09742*.

Better Handling Coreference Resolution in Aspect Level Sentiment Classification by Fine-Tuning Language Models

Dhruv Mullick
Dept. of Computing Science
University of Alberta
mullick@ualberta.ca

Bilal Ghanem
Dept. of Computing Science
University of Alberta
bilalhgm@gmail.com

Alona Fyshe
Dept. of Computing Science
University of Alberta
alona@ualberta.ca

Abstract

Customer feedback is invaluable to companies as they refine their products. Monitoring customer feedback can be automated with Aspect Level Sentiment Classification (ALSC) which allows analyzing specific aspects of the products in reviews. Large Language Models (LLMs) are the heart of many state-of-the-art ALSC solutions, but they perform poorly in some scenarios requiring Coreference Resolution (CR). In this work, we propose a framework to improve an LLM's performance on CR-containing reviews by fine-tuning on highly inferential tasks. We show that the performance improvement is likely attributed to the improved model CR ability. We release a new dataset[1] that focuses on CR in ALSC, and share code[2] for the experiments.

1 Introduction

To understand an end user's perspective on a product, it is common to consider reviews on online platforms. A company can look for the customers' perspective on a certain aspect of the product. For instance, a laptop company might look for reviews concerning "battery." Aspect Level Sentiment Classification (ALSC) analyzes reviews for sentiments of specific aspects, like the "battery" aspect in earlier example (Yan et al., 2021). ALSC is a sub-task of a wider body of work called Aspect Based Sentiment Analysis (ABSA) (Liu, 2012), which aims to extract aspects and their associated sentiments. State-of-the-art ALSC solutions often use Large Language Models (LLMs) (Zhang et al., 2022).

Reviews often use pronouns, which can make coreference resolution (CR) in LLMs necessary to infer the sentiment associated with the aspect. Hence, LLMs used for ALSC need strong CR ability, and can fail otherwise. For instance, the sentence - "*He ate food at the restaurant, it was deserted.*" requires the LLM to understand that the definite pronoun "it" refers to the "restaurant" (antecedent), because of the context ("deserted"). Table 1 shows four examples where the state-of-the-art T5 ALSC model (Zhang et al., 2021) fails due to its poor CR ability. We find that ~15% of this T5 model's errors are on cases requiring CR ability.

Table 1: Cases where the T5 ALSC model fails due to its poor coreference resolution ability.

Sentence	Aspect	Sentiment Polarity	
		Predicted	Gold
He ate food at the restaurant, it was deserted	restaurant	neutral	negative
	food	negative	neutral
He ate food at the restaurant, it was dark	restaurant	neutral	negative
	food	negative	neutral

LLMs are also known to have performance and stability issues (Phang et al., 2018). To remedy these, instead of directly training on the task of interest (target task), it can be beneficial to first train on an auxiliary task (Pruksachatkun et al., 2020). Certain auxiliary tasks can contribute to both improved performance and stability of the target task (Phang et al., 2018). Using auxiliary training, our work shows a way to improve an LLM's performance on English ALSC reviews requiring CR.

In our work, we: **a)** show that an LLM trained for ALSC makes more errors when evaluated only on reviews requiring CR ability, compared to when handling typical ALSC reviews (8.7% mean F1); **b)** demonstrate that our framework for handling CR-containing reviews can improve ALSC model's CR ability (16% mean F1); **c)** show that this improved CR ability can improve ALSC performance for reviews requiring CR ability (5% mean F1). **d)** release annotated variants of existing datasets which can be used to benchmark a model's ALSC performance on CR cases.

[1] https://borealisdata.ca/dataset.xhtml?persistentId=doi:10.5683/SP3/HSKJEY

[2] https://github.com/dhruvmullick/absa-cs

Proceedings of the Sixth Workshop on Computational Models of Reference, Anaphora and Coreference (CRAC 2023), pages 39–47
December 6–7, 2023

2 Experimental Setup

2.1 Data

Original ALSC Datasets We consider English ALSC datasets: SemEval Restaurant (Rest16) (Pontiki et al., 2016) and MAMS (Jiang et al., 2019), both of which contain reviews from a similar restaurant domain. Inspired by Yan et al. (2021), ALSC reviews are processed into an input format suitable for our LLM - "[sentence]. aspect: [aspect]". The ground truth output is "positive", "negative" or "neutral". For example, "*$20 for good sushi cannot be beaten. aspect: sushi*" has the ground truth as "positive". We clean datasets as per Appendix C.

CR Cases We identify reviews in the Rest16 and MAMS datasets that contain definite pronouns, and henceforth call these sentences *Pronoun cases*.

Limiting ourselves to the ALSC task described above, we say that a review is a *CR case* if its sentiment requires proper coreference resolution for correct classification. Specifically, *the aspect should be an antecedent of a definite pronoun which is associated with a sentiment polarity*. For example, "He ate food at the restaurant, it was deserted." with aspect: "restaurant" is a CR case. Here, "restaurant" is the antecedent of "it" which is associated with "deserted" and has negative connotations. CR cases are manually selected from Pronoun cases.

ALSC-CR Dataset Our dataset is composed of the original ALSC datasets (Rest16 and MAMS). The testing, however, is done only using CR cases, and we use a combination of Pronoun and Non-Pronoun cases for validation and train sets. Table 2 presents the dataset composition. Better performance on the test dataset will indicate a superior ability to handle CR cases in ALSC.

The train, validation and test sets are of similar, but not identical, distributions. Due to the limited number of CR cases, it is not possible to have train and validation sets composed entirely of CR cases. More details can be found in Appendix D.

2.2 Auxiliary Tasks

We use highly inferential tasks for auxiliary training in our experiments as they generally provide higher improvements for various NLP target tasks (Pruksachatkun et al., 2020). We select two commonsense tasks - Commongen (Lin et al., 2020) and CosmosQA (Huang et al., 2019), as commonsense reasoning helps with CR (Liu et al., 2017). SQuAD (Rajpurkar et al., 2016) is selected because it is a non-commonsense question answering (QA) task. Its performance is contrasted with CosmosQA, checking if it is the QA or the commonsense ability which improves CR. Quora Question Prediction (Wang et al., 2018) (QQP) is selected as it benefits performance on the Stanford Sentiment Treebank (SST) task which is similar to ALSC (Wang et al., 2019). Even if auxiliary tasks aren't designed for CR, they can impart CR ability to the model. For the QA example - "Context: Alice can't come. She is old"; "Question: Who is old?", answer is "Alice". Answering this requires CR and teaches the model CR ability.

Commongen is a generative commonsense task involving sentence generation from a list of concepts (train size = 67,389). It tests: 1) ability to construct grammatical sentences adhering to commonsense; 2) reasoning with unseen concept combinations. For example: input - "concepts = [dog, frisbee, catch]"; output - "A dog leaps to catch a frisbee."

CosmosQA is a QA task where answering questions requires commonsense (train size = 25,262). For each question, there are four options, and the model should output the correct option number.

SQuAD is an extractive QA task where the correct answer to the question is present exactly in the passage (train size = 87,599).

QQP task involves checking if two Quora questions are semantically equivalent. We cap the train size at 50,000 to match the other datasets.

3 Experiments and Results

We ran experiments for three purposes: **a)** to show there is drop in ALSC performance for reviews requiring CR ability; **b)** to show we can alleviate this performance drop by auxiliary fine-tuning; **c)** to provide additional evidence that change in performance on CR cases is due to improved CR ability.

Inspired by state-of-the-art performance in Zhang et al. (2021), we used the T5 LLM (Raffel et al., 2019). Our baseline model is a T5 trained on ALSC-CR, but not fine-tuned on auxiliary tasks.

The T5 model was trained in various settings using training prompts/input prefixes (Appendix F). Wording of prompts has limited impact on the outcome so we did not experiment with the wording (Raffel et al., 2019). Rather, we relied on prior work for task prompts (Lin et al., 2020; Lourie et al., 2021; Raffel et al., 2019). For ALSC and

Table 2: ALSC-CR composition. Note that CR cases are types of Pronoun cases.

Partition	Size	Dataset		Data Type		
				Pronoun Cases		*Non-Pronoun Cases*
		MAMS	Rest16	CR Cases	Non-CR Pronoun Cases	
Train	12,434	✓	✓	✓	✓	✓
Validation	889	✓	✓	✓	✓	✓
Test	346	✓	✓	✓	✗	✗

Definite Pronoun Resolution (DPR) (Rahman and Ng, 2012) (Sec. 3.3), we created prompts as we did not find examples in prior work (see Appendix F).

All experiments were run with at least 10 random seeds, and Yuen-Welch test was used for testing statistical significance.

3.1 Model Performance on ALSC Without Auxiliary Fine Tuning

To check LLM performance on CR cases, we evaluated the T5 model on regular ALSC data (ALSC-Regular), which does not consist solely of CR cases. ALSC-Regular and ALSC-CR are equal sized and have an identical proportion of Rest16 and MAMS. We also evaluated the T5 model on ALSC-CR, to get the model's performance solely on CR cases.

By comparing T5 model's performance on the two ALSC datasets, we show that unspecialized LLMs face a significant performance problem while handling reviews requiring CR ability. Results are shown in Table 3, where evaluation on ALSC-CR shows a drop in performance of ~8.7% mean F1, as well as an increase of 0.6 F1 standard deviation indicating a poorer model convergence.

Table 3: T5 model evaluated on ALSC datasets. Best score bolded. Performances on the datasets are statistically significantly different (p-value=$9.03e-05$).

Dataset	Mean F1 ($\pm$ Std. Dev)
ALSC-Regular	**79.71** ($\pm$ 1.99)
ALSC-CR	71.07 ($\pm$ 2.60)

3.2 Fine Tuning With Auxiliary Tasks

As a solution to poor performance on ALSC-CR (Section 3.1), we experimented with various auxiliary tasks mentioned in Section 2.2.

We trained T5 model on the auxiliary task first to incorporate auxiliary task knowledge. This model is then trained and evaluated on ALSC-CR, our target task. We experimented with different auxiliary dataset sizes as the size has little correlation with the target task performance (Wang et al., 2019).

The model's performance on ALSC-CR with different auxiliary tasks is compared to baseline model's ALSC-CR performance to see if auxiliary tasks were beneficial. Results are shown in Table 4. We find that the lower ALSC-CR performance (compared to ALSC-Regular) can be alleviated by auxiliary training with Commongen and QQP, which lead to statistically significant improvements of ~5% mean F1. Auxiliary training with CosmosQA and SQuAD does not lead to statistically significant improvement in any case.

Prior work (Pruksachatkun et al., 2020) showed a general improvement in a model's target task performance when fine-tuned with highly inferential tasks. Apart from being highly inferential, because Commongen is a generative commonsense task, it is ideal for imparting commonsense knowledge to a generative LLM like T5. On the other hand, CosmosQA being a discriminative task is unlikely to impart as much commonsense knowledge into a generative system (Lin et al., 2020). As being highly inferential is helpful for target tasks, the SQuAD extractive QA task, would not result in as significant an improvement. When used for auxiliary training, QQP shows a high improvement in the SST target task (Wang et al., 2019) which involves similar sentiment analysis, explaining QQP's improved performance on ALSC-CR.

While auxiliary training on DPR appears promising, its dataset (train size = 1500) is much smaller than for other tasks. For completeness we did train using DPR but the mean F1 = 72.77 was not statistically significantly different from the baseline.

Similar to Wang et al. (2019), we do not find correlation between auxiliary task size and target performance. This lack of correlation may be due to the fact that small datasets might not teach the task sufficiently (Raffel et al., 2019). On the other hand, large auxiliary datasets can cause catastrophic forgetting of the LLM's original objective (Wang et al., 2019). This original objective is generally beneficial for target tasks. Despite this lack of correlation, we have demonstrated a framework for improving

Table 4: Mean F1 (± Std. Dev) performance on ALSC-CR on different fractions of aux dataset. * denotes statistically significant difference from baseline. Table's best scores bolded, 2nd best underlined.

Aux. Task	Aux. Dataset Fraction			
	0.1	**0.2**	**0.5**	**1.0**
Commongen	<u>75.72</u> (± 1.14) *	72.46 (± 2.21)	71.04 (± 3.50)	71.45 (± 1.91)
CosmosQA	71.79 (± 1.55)	71.45 (± 3.02)	72.60 (± 1.85)	73.12 (± 2.15)
SQuAD	72.02 (± 1.88)	72.60 (± 2.07)	71.47 (± 3.24)	72.08 (± 2.25)
QQP	72.49 (± 2.79)	71.85 (± 2.98)	**76.10** (± 1.26) *	71.30 (± 2.19)
N/A (Baseline)	71.07 (± 2.60)			

any target task's performance on CR cases.

We show a pronoun error analysis in Appendix E to better understand the ALSC-CR improvements.

3.3 Evaluating Coreference Ability

Performing well on ALSC-CR requires strong CR ability, as CR associates the aspect with its sentiment. To verify that the improvement in Section 3.2 is attributable to the ALSC model's improved CR ability, we estimate the CR ability by evaluating on DPR. Since we have an ALSC model for each random seed used for training (Section 3.2), we run DPR evaluation on the ALSC random seed model with the highest ALSC-CR val set performance.

DPR involves predicting the antecedent of a given pronoun. This is precisely the ability required for good performance on ALSC-CR (which contains only definite pronoun cases), making DPR ideal to measure the CR ability of models. Other CR datasets like OntoNotes (Hovy et al., 2006), Winograd Schema Challenge (WSC) (Levesque et al., 2012) and WinoGrande (Sakaguchi et al., 2021) are not as suitable as DPR because DPR only focuses on definite pronouns, which is the ability we are interested in. Similarly, DPR is also the only CR dataset suitable for auxiliary training, but the size makes this infeasible as discussed in Section 3.2.

We use a DPR variant for generative models where input is of the form: "Humans were afraid of robots as *they* were strong.", and the objective is to predict what the highlighted pronoun (*they*) is referring to (Raffel et al., 2019).

Evaluating ALSC models on DPR (Table 5) confirms that the ALSC-CR performance gains may be attributable to the improved CR ability of the model due to auxiliary fine-tuning. Experiments show that Commongen and QQP fine-tuned models show a drastically improved (and statistically significant) CR ability of up to ~16%. This explains their improved ALSC-CR performance. Using CosmosQA, we see a statistically significant ~5% deterioration in CR ability which does not lead to statistically significant changes in ALSC-CR performance.

Table 5: CR ability of top performing models (Sec 3.2) measured using DPR. Statistically significant improvement(*) and deterioration(†) from baseline marked. Best bolded, 2nd best underlined.

Aux Task	Aux Frac.	Mean F1 (± Std. Dev)
N/A (Baseline)	0	59.28 (± 8.82)
Commongen	0.1	<u>75.77</u> (± 1.68)*
CosmosQA	1.0	54.55 (± 7.19)†
SQuAD	0.2	62.91 (± 6.77)
QQP	0.5	**76.36** (± 2.16)*

4 Related Work

Prior work notes CR to be important to ABSA and similar tasks (Kobayashi and Malon, 2022; Atkinson and Escudero, 2022). Ding and Liu (2010) use aspect sentiments for performing CR, demonstrating a correlation between CR and sentiment classification. De Clercq and Hoste (2020); De Bruyne et al. (2022) examine CR for detecting aspects from related reviews or images, for the reviews lacking explicit aspects. Instead, we consider an LLM's intra-sentence CR ability, considering only reviews with explicit aspects as having an aspect is critical to ALSC. Mai and Zhang (2020) use CR in aspect extraction, but only for identifying duplicate references among proposed aspects. Varghese and Jayasree (2013) use CR to solve their dependency parser's inability to correctly associate opinion words with pronouns. In our work, we consider the CR problem in end-to-end state-of-the-art ALSC LLM models. Chen et al. (2020) improve BERT LLM's CR ability for opinion-mining, using a method relying on external knowledge bases.

5 Conclusion

Since real-world reviews vary widely, we need ALSC models which can handle various kinds of reviews, including those requiring CR. Although LLMs generally perform well on ALSC, our experiments provide evidence that LLMs can have poor performance on ALSC reviews requiring CR ability. We show that this problem can be alleviated by fine-tuning with certain auxiliary tasks before fine-tuning on the target tasks. Our framework for evaluating and improving an LLM's performance on CR cases can be applied for other tasks as well. Such a framework is critical for developing any model deployed in the real world. In the future, we will explore if auxiliary training can reduce the target task training that is needed for CR cases.

Limitations

- Even though we have successfully demonstrated a framework to handle CR-containing reviews by using auxiliary fine-tuning, we have not found which auxiliary tasks to definitively use for target tasks other than ALSC. The auxiliary task must be found using the framework proposed in our work.

- Our test set is composed of ~350 manually identified examples are guaranteed to require CR ability. However, it is common for ALSC datasets to be small. The bench-marking datasets Twitter, Lap14, Rest16 and Rest15 all have ~500-600 aspects for analysis (Zhang et al., 2019) which is close to our dataset. To reduce the variability due to a relatively small test set, we use multiple random seeds for robustness (Clark et al., 2020).

  Due to the specific problem we are targeting, it is difficult to create more examples than this using existing sources. During qualitative analysis, we had considered many ALSC datasets (SemEval datasets, Twitter, MAMS) but found that the CR problem was most pronounced in the restaurant domain (Rest16, MAMS). Example: laptop reviews rarely use explicit aspects (Pontiki et al., 2014), leading to few CR cases in Lap14 dataset.

- Ours is the first work to demonstrate this CR problem in language models, thus there are few benchmarks against which we can compare our solution.

- We use the T5-large LLM for our experiments which requires a significant amount of computational resources for training. This leads to a high cost both financially and environmentally (Strubell et al., 2019).

References

John Atkinson and Alex Escudero. 2022. Evolutionary natural-language coreference resolution for sentiment analysis. *International Journal of Information Management Data Insights*, 2(2):100115.

Jiahua Chen, Shuai Wang, Sahisnu Mazumder, and Bing Liu. 2020. A knowledge-driven approach to classifying object and attribute coreferences in opinion mining. In *Findings of the Association for Computational Linguistics: EMNLP 2020*, pages 1616–1626, Online. Association for Computational Linguistics.

Kevin Clark, Minh-Thang Luong, Quoc V Le, and Christopher D Manning. 2020. Electra: Pre-training text encoders as discriminators rather than generators. *arXiv preprint arXiv:2003.10555*.

Luna De Bruyne, Akbar Karimi, Orphee De Clercq, Andrea Prati, and Veronique Hoste. 2022. Aspect-based emotion analysis and multimodal coreference: A case study of customer comments on adidas Instagram posts. In *Proceedings of the Thirteenth Language Resources and Evaluation Conference*, pages 574–580, Marseille, France. European Language Resources Association.

Orphee De Clercq and Veronique Hoste. 2020. It's absolutely divine! can fine-grained sentiment analysis benefit from coreference resolution? In *Proceedings of the Third Workshop on Computational Models of Reference, Anaphora and Coreference*, pages 11–21, Barcelona, Spain (online). Association for Computational Linguistics.

Xiaowen Ding and Bing Liu. 2010. Resolving object and attribute coreference in opinion mining. In *Proceedings of the 23rd International Conference on Computational Linguistics (Coling 2010)*, pages 268–276, Beijing, China. Coling 2010 Organizing Committee.

Eduard Hovy, Mitchell Marcus, Martha Palmer, Lance Ramshaw, and Ralph Weischedel. 2006. OntoNotes: The 90% solution. In *Proceedings of the Human Language Technology Conference of the NAACL, Companion Volume: Short Papers*, pages 57–60, New York City, USA. Association for Computational Linguistics.

Lifu Huang, Ronan Le Bras, Chandra Bhagavatula, and Yejin Choi. 2019. Cosmos QA: Machine reading comprehension with contextual commonsense reasoning. In *Proceedings of the 2019 Conference on Empirical Methods in Natural Language Processing and the 9th International Joint Conference on Natural Language Processing (EMNLP-IJCNLP)*, pages 2391–2401, Hong Kong, China. Association for Computational Linguistics.

Qingnan Jiang, Lei Chen, Ruifeng Xu, Xiang Ao, and Min Yang. 2019. A challenge dataset and effective models for aspect-based sentiment analysis. In *Proceedings of the 2019 Conference on Empirical Methods in Natural Language Processing and the*

9th International Joint Conference on Natural Language Processing (EMNLP-IJCNLP)*, pages 6280–6285, Hong Kong, China. Association for Computational Linguistics.

Hideo Kobayashi and Christopher Malon. 2022. Analyzing coreference and bridging in product reviews. In *Proceedings of the Fifth Workshop on Computational Models of Reference, Anaphora and Coreference*, pages 22–30, Gyeongju, Republic of Korea. Association for Computational Linguistics.

Hector Levesque, Ernest Davis, and Leora Morgenstern. 2012. The winograd schema challenge. In *Thirteenth international conference on the principles of knowledge representation and reasoning*.

Bill Yuchen Lin, Wangchunshu Zhou, Ming Shen, Pei Zhou, Chandra Bhagavatula, Yejin Choi, and Xiang Ren. 2020. CommonGen: A constrained text generation challenge for generative commonsense reasoning. In *Findings of the Association for Computational Linguistics: EMNLP 2020*, pages 1823–1840, Online. Association for Computational Linguistics.

Bing Liu. 2012. *Sentiment Analysis and Opinion Mining*. Morgan & Claypool Publishers.

Quan Liu, Hui Jiang, Zhen-Hua Ling, Xiaodan Zhu, Si Wei, and Yu Hu. 2017. Combing context and commonsense knowledge through neural networks for solving winograd schema problems. In *2017 AAAI Spring Symposium Series*.

Nicholas Lourie, Ronan Le Bras, Chandra Bhagavatula, and Yejin Choi. 2021. Unicorn on rainbow: A universal commonsense reasoning model on a new multitask benchmark. *AAAI*.

Deon Mai and Wei Emma Zhang. 2020. Aspect extraction using coreference resolution and unsupervised filtering. In *Proceedings of the 1st Conference of the Asia-Pacific Chapter of the Association for Computational Linguistics and the 10th International Joint Conference on Natural Language Processing: Student Research Workshop*, pages 124–129, Suzhou, China. Association for Computational Linguistics.

Jason Phang, Thibault Févry, and Samuel R Bowman. 2018. Sentence encoders on stilts: Supplementary training on intermediate labeled-data tasks. *arXiv preprint arXiv:1811.01088*.

Maria Pontiki, Dimitris Galanis, Haris Papageorgiou, Ion Androutsopoulos, Suresh Manandhar, Mohammad AL-Smadi, Mahmoud Al-Ayyoub, Yanyan Zhao, Bing Qin, Orphée De Clercq, Véronique Hoste, Marianna Apidianaki, Xavier Tannier, Natalia Loukachevitch, Evgeniy Kotelnikov, Nuria Bel, Salud María Jiménez-Zafra, and Gülşen Eryiğit. 2016. SemEval-2016 task 5: Aspect based sentiment analysis. In *Proceedings of the 10th International Workshop on Semantic Evaluation (SemEval-2016)*, pages 19–30, San Diego, California. Association for Computational Linguistics.

Maria Pontiki, Dimitris Galanis, John Pavlopoulos, Harris Papageorgiou, Ion Androutsopoulos, and Suresh Manandhar. 2014. SemEval-2014 task 4: Aspect based sentiment analysis. In *Proceedings of the 8th International Workshop on Semantic Evaluation (SemEval 2014)*, pages 27–35, Dublin, Ireland. Association for Computational Linguistics.

Yada Pruksachatkun, Jason Phang, Haokun Liu, Phu Mon Htut, Xiaoyi Zhang, Richard Yuanzhe Pang, Clara Vania, Katharina Kann, and Samuel R. Bowman. 2020. Intermediate-task transfer learning with pretrained language models: When and why does it work? In *Proceedings of the 58th Annual Meeting of the Association for Computational Linguistics*, pages 5231–5247, Online. Association for Computational Linguistics.

Colin Raffel, Noam Shazeer, Adam Roberts, Katherine Lee, Sharan Narang, Michael Matena, Yanqi Zhou, Wei Li, and Peter J Liu. 2019. Exploring the limits of transfer learning with a unified text-to-text transformer. *arXiv preprint arXiv:1910.10683*.

Altaf Rahman and Vincent Ng. 2012. Resolving complex cases of definite pronouns: The Winograd schema challenge. In *Proceedings of the 2012 Joint Conference on Empirical Methods in Natural Language Processing and Computational Natural Language Learning*, pages 777–789, Jeju Island, Korea. Association for Computational Linguistics.

Pranav Rajpurkar, Jian Zhang, Konstantin Lopyrev, and Percy Liang. 2016. SQuAD: 100,000+ questions for machine comprehension of text. In *Proceedings of the 2016 Conference on Empirical Methods in Natural Language Processing*, pages 2383–2392, Austin, Texas. Association for Computational Linguistics.

Keisuke Sakaguchi, Ronan Le Bras, Chandra Bhagavatula, and Yejin Choi. 2021. Winogrande: An adversarial winograd schema challenge at scale. *Communications of the ACM*, 64(9):99–106.

Emma Strubell, Ananya Ganesh, and Andrew McCallum. 2019. Energy and policy considerations for deep learning in NLP. In *Proceedings of the 57th Annual Meeting of the Association for Computational Linguistics*, pages 3645–3650, Florence, Italy. Association for Computational Linguistics.

Duyu Tang, Bing Qin, and Ting Liu. 2016. Aspect level sentiment classification with deep memory network. In *Proceedings of the 2016 Conference on Empirical Methods in Natural Language Processing*, pages 214–224, Austin, Texas. Association for Computational Linguistics.

Yuanhe Tian, Guimin Chen, and Yan Song. 2021. Aspect-based sentiment analysis with type-aware graph convolutional networks and layer ensemble. In *Proceedings of the 2021 Conference of the North American Chapter of the Association for Computational Linguistics: Human Language Technologies*, pages 2910–2922, Online. Association for Computational Linguistics.

Raisa Varghese and M Jayasree. 2013. Aspect based sentiment analysis using support vector machine classifier. In *2013 international conference on advances in computing, communications and informatics (ICACCI)*, pages 1581–1586. IEEE.

Alex Wang, Jan Hula, Patrick Xia, Raghavendra Pappagari, R. Thomas McCoy, Roma Patel, Najoung Kim, Ian Tenney, Yinghui Huang, Katherin Yu, Shuning Jin, Berlin Chen, Benjamin Van Durme, Edouard Grave, Ellie Pavlick, and Samuel R. Bowman. 2019. Can you tell me how to get past sesame street? sentence-level pretraining beyond language modeling. In *Proceedings of the 57th Annual Meeting of the Association for Computational Linguistics*, pages 4465–4476, Florence, Italy. Association for Computational Linguistics.

Alex Wang, Amanpreet Singh, Julian Michael, Felix Hill, Omer Levy, and Samuel Bowman. 2018. GLUE: A multi-task benchmark and analysis platform for natural language understanding. In *Proceedings of the 2018 EMNLP Workshop BlackboxNLP: Analyzing and Interpreting Neural Networks for NLP*, pages 353–355, Brussels, Belgium. Association for Computational Linguistics.

Hang Yan, Junqi Dai, Tuo Ji, Xipeng Qiu, and Zheng Zhang. 2021. A unified generative framework for aspect-based sentiment analysis. In *Proceedings of the 59th Annual Meeting of the Association for Computational Linguistics and the 11th International Joint Conference on Natural Language Processing (Volume 1: Long Papers)*, pages 2416–2429, Online. Association for Computational Linguistics.

Chen Zhang, Qiuchi Li, and Dawei Song. 2019. Aspect-based sentiment classification with aspect-specific graph convolutional networks. In *Proceedings of the 2019 Conference on Empirical Methods in Natural Language Processing and the 9th International Joint Conference on Natural Language Processing (EMNLP-IJCNLP)*, pages 4568–4578, Hong Kong, China. Association for Computational Linguistics.

Wenxuan Zhang, Xin Li, Yang Deng, Lidong Bing, and Wai Lam. 2021. Towards generative aspect-based sentiment analysis. In *Proceedings of the 59th Annual Meeting of the Association for Computational Linguistics and the 11th International Joint Conference on Natural Language Processing (Volume 2: Short Papers)*, pages 504–510, Online. Association for Computational Linguistics.

Wenxuan Zhang, Xin Li, Yang Deng, Lidong Bing, and Wai Lam. 2022. A survey on aspect-based sentiment analysis: Tasks, methods, and challenges. *arXiv preprint arXiv:2203.01054*.

A Hyperparameters

Learning rates for both auxiliary fine-tuning and ALSC training steps are picked from $\{5e-4, 1e-4, 5e-5\}$ and $\{1e-3, 5e-4, 1e-4\}$ respectively, after running for three random seeds and selecting the rates giving max F1 score for their respective validation dataset. For auxiliary fine-tuning, the learning rates for all auxiliary tasks were found to be $1e-4$, except for SQuAD with Aux Fraction as 1.0 for which we found learning rate as $5e-5$. For ALSC target task training, the learning rate was found to be $5e-4$ in all cases except when using Commongen task for fine tuning with Aux Fraction as 0.1 for which we found learning rate as $1e-4$.

Batch size for training is taken as 16 to maximize GPU utilization. We train for 30 epochs to allow for convergence, while using an early stopping mechanism.

B Model Details

For our LLM, we use the T5-large implementation on Huggingface.[3]

C Dataset Cleanup

Following existing work (Tang et al., 2016; Tian et al., 2021) we disregard reviews with no aspects, and also the aspects labeled as having "conflict" sentiment polarity to prevent a class imbalance problem due to low count of "conflict" class.

D Dataset Details

Here we present some more details of the ALSC-CR dataset. The aspect polarity distribution is presented in Table 6. Note that it is possible to have multiple pronouns in each of the CR cases.

The sentiment distribution of ALSC-CR test set is shown in Table 7.

For constructing ALSC-CR, we use standard ALSC datasets (MAMS and Rest16). MAMS's original train set along with data from Rest16 train set is used for training. For validation, we use the original validation sets from MAMS and Rest16, in addition to Pronoun cases from MAMS test and Rest16. The composition of the validation dataset is such that we use minimal Pronoun cases for validation while having sufficient CR cases for testing. Details of the composition of ALSC-CR are shown in Table 9.

[3] https://huggingface.co/t5-large

Table 6: Sentiment polarity distribution in ALSC-CR dataset

Partition	Polarity		
	Positive	Negative	Neutral
Train	4,279	3,065	5,090
Validation	337	222	330
Test	178	122	46

Table 7: Pronoun distribution in ALSC-CR test set, which has only CR cases

Pronoun	Count
it	132
which	59
they	54
he	24
who	19
she	17
their	14
them	12
its	10
his	10
there	10
him	5
her	5
hers	0

E Error Analysis by Pronoun

We analyze the errors and improvements seen for individual pronouns (in reviews) when ALSC-CR is evaluated with different ALSC models. Since a few pronouns have very low counts as per Table 7, we only analyze the ones which have count greater than 15.

For all pronouns analyzed, we find improvements in prediction accuracy for the models fine-tuned with auxiliary tasks, compared to the baseline model which has no auxiliary fine-tuning. Results are shown in Table 8.

F Training Prompts

We present the training prompts used in Table 10.

G Visualising Auxiliary Training Results

In Figure 1, we visually show the performance of auxiliary trained models on ALSC-CR (same results as Table 4). We can see that there is little correlation between the auxiliary dataset fraction and the mean F1 performance, making it necessary to explore various fraction settings.

H Training Details

For fine tuning the T5-large model, we use 1 NVIDIA V100 GPU, 6 CPU cores with 4 GB memory per core. We run training jobs with a 71 hour time limit.

Table 8: Error Analysis of ALSC models by pronoun distribution. Model Accuracy% presented by Pronoun. Highest scores bolded. 2nd highest underlined. Pronouns with count less than 15 (as per Table 7) are not analyzed.

Pronoun	Baseline	Commongen 0.1	QQP 0.5
it	65.91	68.18	**71.21**
which	74.58	**83.05**	77.97
they	72.22	**79.63**	77.78
he	70.83	**75.0**	70.83
who	84.21	**94.74**	**94.74**
she	88.24	**94.12**	88.24
their	64.29	78.57	78.57
them	75.0	75.0	75.0
its	80.0	70.0	90.0
his	100.0	100.0	100.0
there	60.0	70.0	60.0
him	60.0	60.0	60.0
her	100.0	100.0	80.0
hers	N/A	N/A	N/A

Figure 1: Performance of ALSC models with aux training on ALSC-CR dataset.

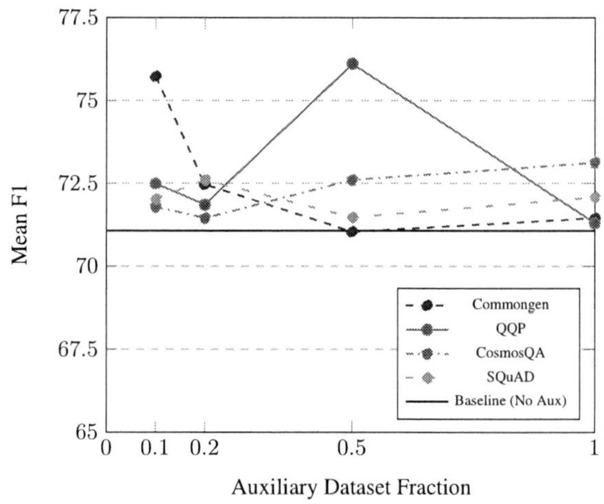

Table 9: Detailed ALSC-CR dataset composition.

Partition	Size	Composition
Train	12,434	MAMS Train (#count = 11,186) + Rest16 Train (Non Pronoun) (#count = 1,248)
Val	889	15% of (MAMS Test (Pronoun) + Rest16 Train/Val/Test (Pronoun)) + 50% of (MAMS Val + Rest Val (Non Pronoun)) [Here, MAMS #count = 746, Rest16 #count = 143]
Test	346	MAMS Test (CR) (#count = 124) + Rest16 Train/Val/Test (CR cases) (#count = 222)

Table 10: Details of T5 training prompts used for auxiliary and target tasks.

Task	Training Prompt
ALSC-CR	get sentiment: [sentence, aspect]
ALSC-Regular	get sentiment: [sentence, aspect]
DPR	Get antecedent: [sentence]
Commongen	generate a sentence with: [concepts]
CosmosQA	question: [question] answer_0: [ans_0] answer_1: [ans_1] answer_2: [ans_2] answer_3: [ans_3] context: [context]
SQuAD	question: [question] context: [context]
QQP	qqp question1: [question_1] question2: [question_2]

The Pragmatics of Characters' Mental Perspectives in Pronominal Reference Resolution

Tiana V. Simovic
University of Toronto
tiana.simovic@mail.utoronto.ca

Craig G. Chambers
University of Toronto
craig.chambers@utoronto.ca

Abstract

To date, cognitive models of pronoun resolution have primarily focused on how fairly shallow discourse-level and lexical cues yield the appropriate interpretation, despite classic work in computational linguistics emphasizing the importance of situation-specific pragmatic reasoning. We explore the latter in two studies of human judgments, which highlight the striking robustness of these pragmatic processes.

1 Introduction

Models of pronoun resolution are typically built around comparatively "shallow" heuristics such as discourse-level cues (e.g., first-mention cues, focus tracking, "Centering" (Grosz et al., 1995)) and lexical cues derived from semantic aspects of the verb (e.g., so-called "implicit causality"). These cues are readily implemented in both small- and large-scale models and have been pursued with the hope that these models would achieve high accuracy without the need to incorporate rich knowledge postulates and pragmatic reasoning. Work in psycholinguistics has reflected this same focus, with the majority of studies exploring how discourse-level and lexical cues guide human intuitions about referent identity (Kaiser and Fedele, 2019). This work has often concluded that discourse/lexical cues provide a kind of rapid default interpretation, as reflected by statistical tendencies in human judgments. Interestingly, this shared approach fails to capture many important insights from classic work in computational linguistics, which highlighted how situation-specific pragmatic reasoning is essential for resolving pronouns in many circumstances (e.g., Winograd, 1972; Hobbs, 1979; Hobbs et al., 1993). Given that cases involving situational reasoning are often described as challenging for computational models (e.g., Levesque et al., 2012; Sakaguchi et al., 2021), and are often incompatible with the solution yielded by default bias, it is possible that they are also difficult for humans to interpret. This would be reflected in less robust judgments compared to cases where pragmatic inferencing is not necessary for accurate identification of the intended referent. However, consider the following example from Jones and Bergen (2021):

(1) a. When the vase fell on the rock, it broke.
b. When the rock fell on the vase, it broke.

A resolution account based on shallow cues would predict that the pronoun *it* should resolve to the subject antecedent in both (1a-b). However, Jones and Bergen found that human readers judge the object-position antecedent (*vase*) in (1b) as the intended referent 95% of the time (e.g., despite that antecedent's status as the second-mentioned and therefore less "focal/centered" entity). This finding highlights how readers draw on world knowledge – something that continues to be difficult to integrate into current models of anaphora resolution (Richard-Bollans et al., 2018).

The present study extends the psycholinguistic work on inference in pronoun resolution by exploring how another form of world knowledge, namely mentalizing and perspective-taking about story characters, guides human pronoun resolution. This line of work provides challenging test cases for state-of-the-art computational models of coreference resolution in English.

2 Experiment 1: Subject Pronoun judgment Task

The first experiment (54 adult participants, M_{age}=34.54 years, SD_{age}=12.8, recruited from Prolific [www.prolific.com]; 24 critical trials) focused on *subject*-position pronouns using short sentences like in (2):

(2) a. Madeline told Anna that she remembers when the lecture starts.

Proceedings of the Sixth Workshop on Computational Models of Reference, Anaphora and Coreference (CRAC 2023), pages 48–50
December 6–7, 2023

b. Madeline asked Anna if she remembers when the lecture starts.

We predicted that a character *telling* an interlocutor about the information expressed in the subordinate clause should lead readers to interpret the pronoun as coreferring with the main-clause subject, whereas *asking* should entail main-clause object selections. This is because (in relation to the examples in (2)) we do not normally tell people what they remember (conversational contributions should be informative, cf. Grice, 1975), and we do not normally ask people what we ourselves remember (e.g., Brown-Schmidt et al., 2008).

The results overwhelmingly supported these predictions: Participants chose the "perspectivally congruent" antecedent 99.8% of the time. The robustness of this judgment is striking relative to the strength of the patterns observed in computational and psycholinguistic studies exploring the effectiveness of superficial discourse/lexical cues (e.g., Tetreault, 2001; Kehler and Rohde, 2013). Further, there was no order-of-mention bias (which would predict more pronounced effects for *tell*, where the antecedent is the first-mentioned character). Specifically, readers picked the subject antecedent 99.7% of the time in the *tell* sentences and the object antecedent 99.8% of the time in the *ask* sentences. This illustrates that the pragmatic reasoning in question completely overrules the influence of canonical discourse effects related to order-of-mention, which is the pattern otherwise predicted in Centering and most other focus-based models.

3 Experiment 2: Object Pronoun judgment Task

To ensure the patterns are not due to readers drawing on statistical patterns regarding how arguments in a clause containing *tell* or *ask* are linked to a subsequent subject pronoun, we conducted the same experiment with *object* pronouns.

The experiment (54 adult participants, M_{age}=33.83 years, SD_{age}=13.43, recruited from Prolific [`www.prolific.com`]; 24 critical trials) was the same as Experiment 1, except that we now used sentences with object-position pronouns as in (3):

(3) a. Nina told Mary that modern art interests her more than classics.

b. Nina asked Mary if modern art interests her more than classics.

The results reflected the same reasoning-driven patterns as in Experiment 1, with the perspectivally-congruent antecedent selected 99.4% of the time (99% subject antecedent selection in *tell* sentences, and 99.7% object antecedent selection in *ask* sentences). The *ask* case result again demonstrates the apparent dominance of pragmatic reasoning over discourse- and structural-based cues in pronoun resolution.

4 Discussion

The judgment tasks showed extremely robust effects of perspectival inference on pronoun interpretation, suggesting that discourse biases are completely overruled by pragmatic reasoning, consistent with the findings from Jones and Bergen (2021). However, an alternative explanation that might be compatible with minimal use of world knowledge and pragmatic reasoning is that readers are drawing on stored "constructions" of some kind (Goldberg, 1995), as illustrated in (4) and (5):

(4) NP_1 told NP_2 [that] ... $PRONOUN_1$ ...

(5) NP_1 asked NP_2 [if] ... $PRONOUN_2$ ...

However, when we begin extending our consideration of these "perspective" discourses further, it becomes apparent that changes to other aspects of the sentences can strongly shift intuitions:

(6) a. Jane, who noticed it was 12:30 PM, was walking with her good friend Hana.

b. Jane, who is unfamiliar with Japanese currency, was talking to her tour guide, Hana.

c. Jane asked Hana if she had enough cash to buy a sandwich.

(7) a. Susan asked Molly if she likes pie.

b. Little Sue asked her mom if she likes pie.

(8) Max told Gerald that he had lint on the back of his coat.

Our preliminary work shows that when readers are shown either (6a) or (6b) and then prompted for judgments about whom the pronoun *she* refers to in (6c), readers shift from choosing the subject antecedent 12.5% of the time in (6a) to 100% of the time in (6b), suggesting the context provided in (6b) overrides typical *ask* selections by encouraging a different understanding of which character possesses the relevant knowledge (epistemic authority) for the question under discussion. Similarly, although (7a-b) share the same structure and predicates, the understood antecedents clearly shift. The pronoun in sentence (7a) should again follow the pattern we found with our *ask* materials, however, (7b) suggests that Little Sue, who is presumably a child, can be asking her mom whether she herself likes to eat pie. Finally, (8) seems to demonstrate the opposite pattern of our *tell* materials, where the pronoun intuitively corefers with *Gerald*, the object antecedent of the sentence, as this character would be most likely to possess the knowledge in question. Given these examples, which all reflect intelligent perspective reasoning, it is unlikely that reliance on some abstract form of verb-specific frames underlies the observed patterns in the experiments reported above.

In summary, the findings highlight the cost of not including world knowledge and reasoning (cf. Grice, 1975) into current models of pronoun resolution and also underscore the benefit of expanding the standard stock of test cases when creating performance benchmarks for automated systems (Byron, 2003; Webster et al., 2018). We are currently assessing human judgments for cases like (6) and (7) to further test the importance of perspective cues and substantiate the account advanced above that readers' selection patterns are a result of intelligent reasoning and world knowledge rather than a reliance on shallow cues like sentence frames. We hope our work will inform the design of future benchmarks and computational models of anaphora resolution.

Limitations

A limitation of our work is that we only tested a narrow range of experimenter-constructed materials. Future work should extend this analysis to a wider range of materials, including similar cases found in naturalistic corpora.

Further, this work could be extended to languages beyond English that have different anaphoric patterns, such as the occurrence of zero pronouns in Japanese.

References

Sarah Brown-Schmidt, Christine Gunlogson, and Michael K. Tanenhaus. 2008. Addressees distinguish shared from private information when interpreting questions during interactive conversation. *Cognition*, 107(3):1122–1134.

Donna Byron. 2003. Annotation of pronouns and their antecedents: A comparison of two domains. *Technical Report 703, University of Rochester*.

Adele E. Goldberg. 1995. *Constructions: A construction grammar approach to argument structure*. University of Chicago Press.

Herbert P. Grice. 1975. Logic and conversation. In *Speech Acts*, pages 41–58. Brill.

Barbara J. Grosz, Aravind K. Joshi, and Scott Weinstein. 1995. Centering: A framework for modeling the local coherence of discourse. *Computational Linguistics*, 21(2):203–225.

Jerry R. Hobbs. 1979. Coherence and coreference. *Cognitive Science*, 3(1):67–90.

Jerry R. Hobbs, Mark E. Stickel, Douglas E. Appelt, and Paul Martin. 1993. Interpretation as abduction. *Artificial Intelligence*, 63(1–2):69–142.

Cameron R. Jones and Benjamin Bergen. 2021. The role of physical inference in pronoun resolution. In *Proceedings of the 43rd Annual Meeting of the Cognitive Science Society*, volume 43.

Elsi Kaiser and Emily Fedele. 2019. Reference resolution: A psycholinguistic perspective. In Jeanette Gundel and Barbara Abbott, editors, *The Oxford Handbook of Reference*. Oxford University Press.

Andrew Kehler and Hannah Rohde. 2013. A probabilistic reconciliation of coherence-driven and centering-driven theories of pronoun interpretation. *Theoretical Linguistics*, 39(1-2):1–37.

Hector Levesque, Ernest Davis, and Leora Morgenstern. 2012. The Winograd Schema Challenge. In *13th International Conference on the Principles of Knowledge Representation and Reasoning*, pages 552–561.

Adam L. Richard-Bollans, Lucía Gómez Álvarez, and Anthony G. Cohn. 2018. The role of pragmatics in solving the Winograd Schema Challenge. In *Proceedings of the 13th International Symposium on Commonsense Reasoning (Commonsense 2017)*. CEUR Workshop Proceedings.

Keisuke Sakaguchi, Ronan Le Bras, Chandra Bhagavatula, and Yejin Choi. 2021. Winogrande: An adversarial Winograd Schema Challenge at scale. *Communications of the Association for Computing Machinery*, 64(9):99–106.

Joel R. Tetreault. 2001. A corpus-based evaluation of Centering and pronoun resolution. *Computational Linguistics*, 27(4):507–520.

Kellie Webster, Marta Recasens, Vera Axelrod, and Jason Baldridge. 2018. Mind the gap: A balanced corpus of gendered ambiguous pronouns. *Transactions of the Association for Computational Linguistics*, 6:605–617.

Terry Winograd. 1972. Understanding natural language. *Cognitive Psychology*, 3(1):1–191.

MARRS: Multimodal Reference Resolution System

Halim Cagri Ates, Shruti Bhargava[1], Site Li, Jiarui Lu, Siddhardha Maddula, Joel Ruben Antony Moniz[2], Anil Kumar Nalamalapu, Roman Hoang Nguyen, Melis Ozyildirim, Alkesh Patel, Dhivya Piraviperumal[3], Vincent Renkens, Ankit Samal, Thy Tran, Bo-Hsiang Tseng[4], Hong Yu[5], Yuan Zhang, Rong Zou*

{[1]shruti_bhargava, [2]joelmoniz, [3]dhivyaprp, [4]bohsiang_tseng, [5]hong_yu}@apple.com

Apple

Abstract

Successfully handling context is essential for any dialog understanding task. This context maybe be conversational (relying on previous user queries or system responses), visual (relying on what the user sees, for example, on their screen), or background (based on signals such as a ringing alarm or playing music). In this work, we present an overview of MARRS, or Multimodal Reference Resolution System, an on-device framework within a Natural Language Understanding system, responsible for handling conversational, visual and background context. In particular, we present different machine learning models to enable handing contextual queries; specifically, one to enable reference resolution, and one to handle context via query rewriting. We also describe how these models complement each other to form a unified, coherent, lightweight system that can understand context while preserving user privacy.

1 Introduction

Fast-paced advancements across modalities have presented exciting opportunities and daunting challenges for dialogue agents. The ability to seamlessly integrate and interpret different types of information is crucial to achieve human-like understanding. One fundamental aspect of dialogue agents, therefore, is their ability to understand references to context, which is essential to enable them carry out coherent conversations. Traditional reference resolution systems (Yang et al., 2019) are not sufficient for multiple modalities in a dialogue agent.

In this work, we introduce MultimodAl Reference Resolution System (MARRS), targeted to understand and resolve diverse context understanding use cases. MARRS leverages multiple types of context to understand a request, while completely running on-device, keeping memory and privacy as key design factors. The key objective of MARRS is two-fold: first, to track and maintain coherence during multiple turns of a conversation, and second, to leverage visual context to enhance context understanding. It thus aims to provide a centralized domain agnostic solution to diverse discourse and referencing tasks including, but not limited to[1]:

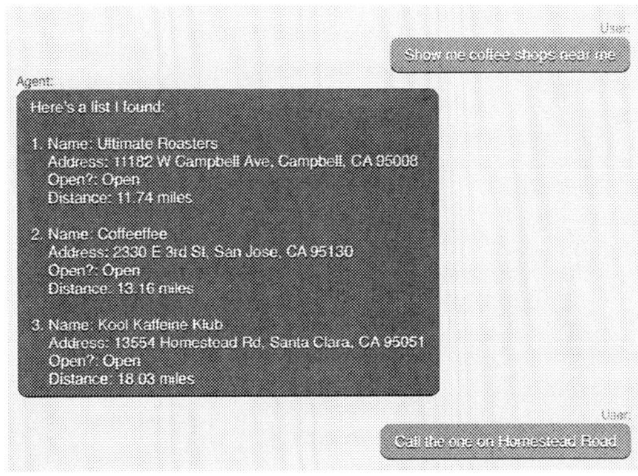

Figure 1: An example of Conversational Entity Resolution. All coffee shop names shown are author-created.

Anaphora Resolution

```
User: What is Ohio's capital?
Agent: Columbus is the capital of Ohio.
User: How far away is it?
```

Ellipsis Resolution

```
User: What is the currency of France?
Agent: The Euro is the currency of France.
User: What about United States?
```

Screen Entity Resolution

```
User: Share this number with John.
```

Conversational Entity Resolution Note that here, the entity may be a part of the interaction without being explicitly mentioned.

```
User: Show me pharmacies near me.
```

*Authors listed in alphabetical order

[1]Examples shown are author-created queries based on anonymized and randomly sampled virtual assistant logs.

Proceedings of the Sixth Workshop on Computational Models of Reference, Anaphora and Coreference (CRAC 2023), pages 51–58
December 6–7, 2023

```
Agent: Here are some near you: <list>
User: Call the second one
```

Background Entity Resolution

```
*alarm starts ringing*
User: Switch it off
```

Correction by Repetition

```
User: What is the population of Australia
Agent: The population of Australia is ...
User: I meant Austria
```

MARRS consumes the transcribed request, and as a part of the language understanding block, aims to allow for fluent conversations spanning multiple modalities. It takes screen entities, conversation history, and other contextual entities as input alongside the latest transcribed request; and outputs a context independent rewritten request as well as spans that link references to entities. In some cases, like *conversational referencing* above, a span with entity id may be preferred by downstream components, while a rewritten query may be preferred in *ellipsis resolution* for transparent low-effort adoption downstream. Central to the success of MARRS are its two components: the query rewriter and the reference resolver (comprising, in turn, of the mention detector and the mention resolver). The query rewriter aims to rewrite a user query to make it context independent, thereby making it self contained. The mention detector and resolver on the other hand aim to generate reference spans.

In this paper, we delve into the system design of MARRS, its components, the reasoning behind them and how they integrate together for efficient context understanding. Note that while we find our system highly efficient and performant, detailed benchmarks and results are outside the scope of this paper. We believe this work will foster an understanding of multimodal context understanding systems and pave the way for more sophisticated and contextually-aware agents.

2 System Design

The context carryover problem is usually tackled with coreference resolution (Ng and Cardie, 2002). Traditional coreference resolution systems often identify mentions and link the mention to entities in the previous context (Lee et al., 2017). Another approach to address the problem is to rewrite the user request into a version which can be executed in a context independent way (Nguyen et al., 2021; Quan et al., 2019; Yu et al., 2020; Tseng et al., 2021). There are pros and cons for each of the two approaches.

On one hand, coreference resolution provides spans with entities, which downstream systems can consume. This removes the need to perform entity linking again, which may add latency and/or errors, and also supports references to complex entities (like calendar events) where rewriting to a natural language query could be hard. On the other hand, the rewrite approach can handle not only the coreference resolution problem, but also other discourse phenomena such as intent carryover, corrections and disfluencies. Further, a coreference resolution system generates spans that need to be adopted by downstream systems, while a rewriting system reformulates the query itself, requiring no explicit adoption. In MARRS, we generate both reference spans and and query rewrites in order to take advantage of both approaches. See Figure 2 for the design of MARRS.

There have been multiple prior works as shown in Table 1, trying to solve different aspects of reference resolution. A real-world dialogue system, however, requires the ability to simultaneous handle all of these aspects. In the MARRS system we do this using 2 major components, the Query Rewriter and the Reference Resolution System. The query rewrite component rewrites the current utterance with previous context, solving problems like anaphora and ellipses. Our reference resolution (or MDMR) component takes in contextual and screen entities and decorates the current utterance with entity information. This helps solve use cases related to screen, background and conversational references. Note that both the Query Rewriter and the Reference Resolution System are independent of each other; consequently, for efficency, they can be run in parallel. Overall, this system consumes dialog context, the current utterance, and entities as input, and produces a rewritten utterance and reference spans as output. Furthermore, the system has been designed to run on the (relatively low-power) device to preserve the privacy of the users.

Within our coreference resolution system, our system runs on *all* user queries, since we do not know a priori if a user query requires resolution. Consequently, while end-to-end approaches have been proposed (Lee et al., 2017), we find it extremely beneficial for system performance to have a 2-stage pipeline: a light-weight Mention Detec-

Previous work on Reference Resolution	Anaphora	Ellipses	Correction by Repetition	Screen Entity Resolution	Conversational Entity Resolution
Bohnet et al. (2023)	✓	✗	✗	✗	✗
Bhargava et al. (2023)	✗	✗	✗	✓	✗
Nguyen et al. (2021)	✗	✗	✓	✗	✗
Tseng et al. (2021)	✓	✓	✗	✗	✗

Table 1: Comparison of previous work on reference resolution covering various use cases

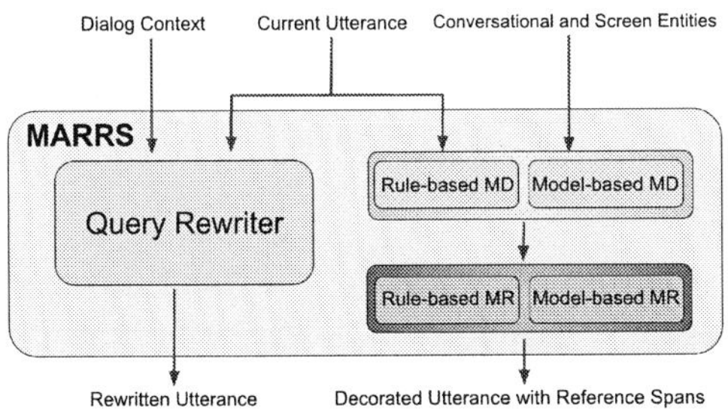

Figure 2: High level diagram show-casing how MARRS models interface with each other

tor (MD), followed by a more expensive Mention Resolver (MR) which is only run if MD detects a mention. We discuss each component in the following sections and detailed model architectures are provided in Section A.1.

2.1 Mention Detector

The Mention Detector (MD) identifies sub-strings in the user utterance that can be grounded to one or more contextual entity. These are also known as referring expressions or mentions. Some examples of referring expressions are:

```
How big is [this house]
Where does [he] live
```

2.1.1 Model-based MD

This predicts which sequences of tokens (spans) need to be resolved to an entity. The model takes in token embeddings and enumerates all spans consisting of start and end token indices. For each span, the first and last token embeddings are concatenated and fed into a feed forward network that performs binary classification. We opt for this approach instead of an LSTM or self-attention based sequence tagger because using a classifier that classifies all spans allows the model the flexibility to identify multiple (possibly overlapping) mentions, while also allowing all spans to be classified independently in parallel (as opposed to sequentially or auto-regressively). Our approach is very similar to that of Lee et al. (2017), except that we empirically observe very little impact by removing the self-attention layer in their mention detector (primarily because our coreference dependencies tend to be much shorter than theirs), while observing very large improvements in both latency and memory. The model architecture is shown in A.1 Figure 3.

2.1.2 Rule-based MD

While the model detects referring expressions (which often include marker words like "this" and "that"), there are cases when the user refers to a contextual entity by name only (omitting the referring expression). In a user request like “Call customer support”, “customer support” might refer to a support number on the user’s screen. To keep the model light-weight, MD model does not consume entities; consequently, it is unable to detect that "customer support" is a referring expression. The Rule-based MD component bridges this gap by matching the gathered contextual entities to the utterance through smart string matching. If a contextual entity is found in the utterance, this subcomponent outputs the span and the corresponding entity as a potential reference.

2.2 Mention Resolver

The Mention Resolver (MR) resolves references in user queries to contextual entities like phone numbers and email addresses. As with the overall system, the focus is on a low memory footprint and reusing the existing components in the pipeline. MR operates on the text and location of screen or conversational entities recognized by upstream component and the metadata of the background entities. It consumes the possible mentions identified by MD and matches each mention to zero, one or more entities, providing a relevance score for each. It includes a mixture of a rule-based system and a machine learned model. The rule-based system is high precision and extremely fast. Consequently, if it outputs a resolution, the model is not run, which yields a substantial latency reduction.

2.2.1 Rule-based MR

Rule-based MR utilizes a set of pre-defined rules and keywords to match references to the correct category, location and text. For example, references like ordinals are matched with regex patterns sorted by the longest match; likewise, music and movie entities can be matched by relying on the presence of verbs like 'play'.

2.2.2 Model-based MR

We also design a modular reference resolution model, inspired by Yu et al. (2018). This is trained to score how well an entity matches with the detected mention. The entities for which score crosses a threshold are then predicted. The model contains 3 modules: 1. the category module, which matches the mention with the entity's category; 2. the location module, which matches the mention with the entity's location; 3. the text module, which matches the mention with the text within entities, like screen texts and alarm names. Weights are computed using the request tokens to determine the aggregation of the the three module scores. We refer interested readers to Bhargava et al. (2023) for a more in-depth understanding of the model; we show the model architecture in Appendix Figure 4.

Screen-based The entities on screen are the candidate referents here. Each entity has a category like phone number and address, a bounding box representing its location on the screen and associated text values. Each of the three modules thus receive input for screen entities, and play a key role in understanding diverse references.

Conversational Here, a user's previous conversational interaction and the VA's responses are considered as referents. In such cases, descriptive references made by a user, such as when referring to addresses (Eg: "Show me coffee shops near me" -> "Call the one on Homestead Road") are to be handled by the text module. The location module is critical in resolving ordinal and spatial references (Eg: "Show me coffee shops near me" -> "Call the bottom one" or "Call the last one").

Background In this case, entities relevant to background tasks are potential referents. These tasks may include user-initiated tasks, such as music that's playing in the background, or system-triggered tasks, such as a ringing alarm or a new notification. The category module is particularly important here, since a user's references tend to be related to the type of the referent (Eg: "pause it" likely refers to music or a movie, while "stop that" could also refer to an alarm or a timer).

2.3 Query Rewriter

The Query Rewriter (QR) is the component that rewrites the last user utterance in a conversation between the user and the VA into a context-free utterance such that it can be fully interpreted and understood without the dialog context. Three use cases mentioned in Section 1 can be tackled through rewriting: Anaphora, Ellipses, and Corrections by Repetition. The output rewritten utterance is provided as an alternative to downstream components together with the original utterance, to provide them with the flexibility of choice.

Again, for the sake of latency and privacy, the QR model is run on device along with MD and MR. Unlike the more complex components in MD and MR, QR is merely an LSTM-based seq2seq model with a copy mechanism (Gu et al., 2016). It takes as input both conversational context (i.e., a sequence of interactions) and the last user query, and generates the rewritten utterance. On top of the encoder, there is a classifier that consumes the input embeddings and predicts the type of use case ('Anaphora and Ellipsis', 'Correction by Repetition' or 'None'). 'None' means no rewriting is required, in which case, to further reduce latency, no decoder inference needs to be run, and the module can simply pass-through the input utterance as the output. This classification signal is also sent as part of the output to downstream systems for their use. The model architecture can be referred to Figure 5 in Appendix.

3 Datasets

Since the system handles varied kinds of references, different datasets are used for training the different components. We briefly describe here the datasets used by the system.

For Screen Entity Resolution, we collect requests referring to entities on screens by showing screenshots containing entities to annotators. One entity is highlighted as the target entity. Annotators are asked to provide requests that refer uniquely to the marked entity. The collected requests are sent through another round of annotation for getting the mentions, in order to train MD. Interested readers can refer to Bhargava et al. (2023) for more details on the data collection. The requests and mentions collected alongside the entities are used to train the model-based MD and MR, as well as to evaluate the overall system.

For Conversational Entity Resolution, we show annotators a list of entities similar to the Agent turn in Figure 1. These lists are synthetically generated based on the domain. Annotators are asked to provide a request referring to any one entity in the list (similar to the second User turn in Figure 1), along with the the mention (to train MD) and the list index of the entity being referred (to train MR).

For Entity Resolution, we additionally have a synthetic data pipeline. Requests are generated through templates like 'play [this]' or 'share [that address] with John', with the marked mention used to train MD. A synthetic list of targeted entities is part of the templates, and synthetic negative entities are added while training MR.

For Query Rewriting, we use mined data from the anonymized opt-in usage data. We first identify the opportunities where user experience can be significantly improved if the desired features are enabled. In particular, for the use case of anaphora and ellipsis, we identify user queries discussing the same entity in two consecutive turns without the use of any referring expressions (context-free query). We then ask annotators to simplify these complex queries to provide queries in a more natural way (context-dependent query). For the use case of correction by repetition, we recognize queries where the user tapped on the transcribed prompt to edit the query into something else. The resulting utterance serves as a complete context-free query. We then prepend the edit parts with common prefixes such as '*I said*' to synthesize the context-dependent query. By doing so, we simulate the pair of original queries and their rewrites for the two desired features. More detailed statistics and examples of both use cases are shown in Appendix A.2 and A.3.

4 Experimental Results

4.1 Metrics

We compute a bag of words token level F1 metric on the subset of tokens that are present in the target

Model	Dataset/Task	F1	EM
QR	AER	91.44	87.83
	CbR	88.12	71.44
MDMR	Screen	83.39	80.8
	Conversational	89.85	91.50
	Synthetic	97.56	96.90

Table 2: Experimental results for QR and MDMR. Here, the Synthetic MDMR dataset tests performance of both Conversational and Background Entity Resolution use-cases.

rewrite, but not in the corresponding context dependent query. This metric reflects the model's ability to carry over tokens from previous context. We also calculate an exact string match accuracy (EM) between the model prediction and the target rewrite as a more strict comparison. Metrics for anaphora and ellipsis resolution (AER) and correction by repetition (CbR) are measured separately.

For reference resolution, metrics are computed by comparing the true target entities with the predicted entities (for which scores cross the threshold). Similar to above, we report F1 and exact match metrics. Here, exact match is 1 if the predicted entities over all predicted references exactly match the true target entities, and is 0 if any additional or missing predicted entities exist.

4.2 Performance

We present an overview of our system performance as measured on the datasets described in Section 3 in Table 2, with additional results in Appendix A.4. We find that our models afford excellent performance despite being extremely small, lightweight enough with respect to both model size and runtime inference latency to potentially deploy them to a low-power device. In particular, the reported results use a QR model with just 4.5M parameters with 1-layer 128-dim LSTMs as encoder and decoder; the MD and MR models are even lighter, with just 116k and 196k parameters respectively.

5 Conclusions

In this paper, we propose and provide a system-level overview of MARRS, a low memory system that combines multiple models to solve context understanding. Our design choices offer an interpretable and agile system. This system can improve user experience in a multi-turn dialogue agent in a fast, efficient, on-device and privacy-preserved manner.

References

Shruti Bhargava, Anand Dhoot, Ing-marie Jonsson, Hoang Long Nguyen, Alkesh Patel, Hong Yu, and Vincent Renkens. 2023. Referring to screen texts with voice assistants. In *Proceedings of the 61st Annual Meeting of the Association for Computational Linguistics (Volume 5: Industry Track)*, pages 752–762, Toronto, Canada. Association for Computational Linguistics.

Bernd Bohnet, Chris Alberti, and Michael Collins. 2023. Coreference resolution through a seq2seq transition-based system. *Transactions of the Association for Computational Linguistics*, 11:212–226.

Jiatao Gu, Zhengdong Lu, Hang Li, and Victor OK Li. 2016. Incorporating copying mechanism in sequence-to-sequence learning. In *Proceedings of the 54th Annual Meeting of the Association for Computational Linguistics (Volume 1: Long Papers)*, pages 1631–1640.

Kenton Lee, Luheng He, Mike Lewis, and Luke Zettlemoyer. 2017. End-to-end neural coreference resolution. In *Proceedings of the 2017 Conference on Empirical Methods in Natural Language Processing*, pages 188–197.

Vincent Ng and Claire Cardie. 2002. Improving machine learning approaches to coreference resolution. In *Proceedings of the 40th annual meeting of the Association for Computational Linguistics*, pages 104–111.

Hoang Long Nguyen, Vincent Renkens, Joris Pelemans, Srividya Pranavi Potharaju, Anil Kumar Nalamalapu, and Murat Akbacak. 2021. User-initiated repetition-based recovery in multi-utterance dialogue systems. *arXiv preprint arXiv:2108.01208*.

Jun Quan, Deyi Xiong, Bonnie Webber, and Changjian Hu. 2019. Gecor: An end-to-end generative ellipsis and co-reference resolution model for task-oriented dialogue. In *Proceedings of the 2019 Conference on Empirical Methods in Natural Language Processing and the 9th International Joint Conference on Natural Language Processing (EMNLP-IJCNLP)*, pages 4547–4557.

Bo-Hsiang Tseng, Shruti Bhargava, Jiarui Lu, Joel Ruben Antony Moniz, Dhivya Piraviperumal, Lin Li, and Hong Yu. 2021. Cread: Combined resolution of ellipses and anaphora in dialogues. In *Proceedings of the 2021 Conference of the North American Chapter of the Association for Computational Linguistics: Human Language Technologies*, pages 3390–3406.

Wei Yang, Rui Qiao, Haocheng Qin, Amy Sun, Luchen Tan, Kun Xiong, and Ming Li. 2019. End-to-end neural context reconstruction in Chinese dialogue. In *Proceedings of the First Workshop on NLP for Conversational AI*, pages 68–76, Florence, Italy. Association for Computational Linguistics.

Licheng Yu, Zhe Lin, Xiaohui Shen, Jimei Yang, Xin Lu, Mohit Bansal, and Tamara L Berg. 2018. Mattnet: Modular attention network for referring expression comprehension. In *Proceedings of the IEEE conference on computer vision and pattern recognition*, pages 1307–1315.

Shi Yu, Jiahua Liu, Jingqin Yang, Chenyan Xiong, Paul Bennett, Jianfeng Gao, and Zhiyuan Liu. 2020. Few-shot generative conversational query rewriting. In *Proceedings of the 43rd International ACM SIGIR Conference on Research and Development in Information Retrieval*, SIGIR '20, page 1933–1936, New York, NY, USA. Association for Computing Machinery.

A Appendix

A.1 Detailed Model Architectures

This section provides the model architectures of MD (Figure 3), MR (Figure 4) and QR (Figure 5) adopted in the MARRS system.

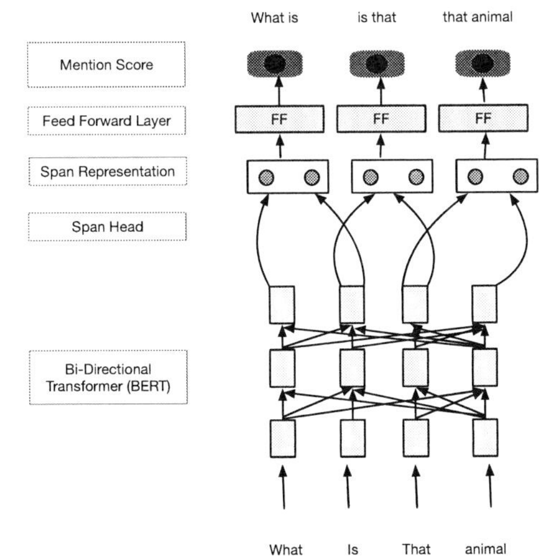

Figure 3: MD model overview

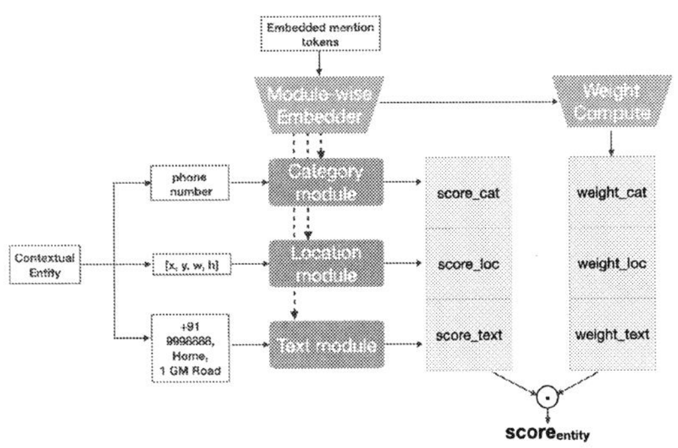

Figure 4: MR model overview

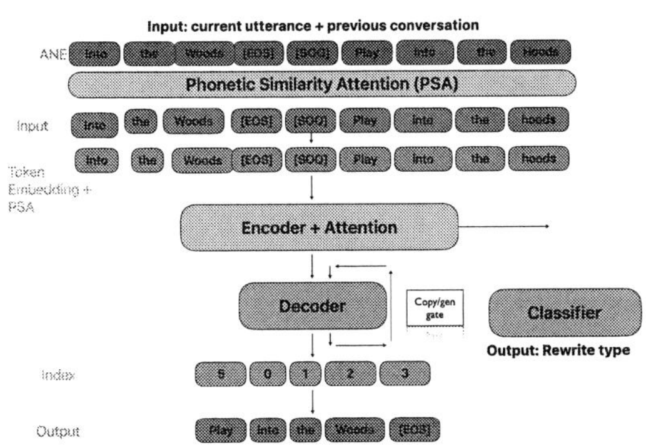

Figure 5: QR model overview

A.2 Data Statistics

Here, we present more detailed statistics around our datasets. In particular, we present the sizes of each dataset: we show how much data was used from each set for training, validation and testing. We present these numbers in Table 3.

Model	Dataset/Task	Train	Val	Test
MDMR	Screen	7.3k	0.7k	1.9k
	Conversational	2.3k	0.4k	1.2k
	Synthetic	3.9k	0.5k	1.1k
QR	AER	300.3k	37.3k	37.2k
	CbR	317.5k	39.7k	39.7k

Table 3: Dataset sizes used for the MDMR and QR models.

A.3 Data Collection

This section provides an example of anaphora, ellipsis and correction by repetition of our data mining methods, as shown in Figure 6.

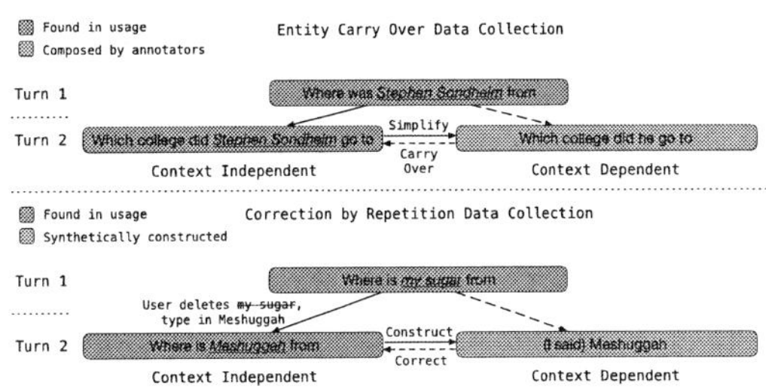

Figure 6: Illustration of data collection process for Anaphora, Ellipses and Correction by Repetition. Examples shown are author-created examples based on anonymized and randomly sampled virtual assistant logs. In both examples, utterances in green are improvement opportunities found in real-world usage, utterances in yellow are either annotated or synthetically generated. During data collection phase, we follow the solid lines. During model training, we follow the dotted lines.

A.4 Results

In this section, we present a deep dive of the results shown in Section 4.1. In particular, we present detailed precision, recall and F1 numbers for our QR, MD and MR models, as well as our joint MDMR performance. Note that in the case of QR, following Quan et al. (2019), we measure the F1 score by comparing generated rewrites and references for only the rewritten part of user utterances. This

Model	Dataset/Task	P	R	F1
MD	Screen	89.66	95.74	92.60
	Conversational	85.30	92.60	88.80
	Synthetic	99.00	99.70	99.30
MR	Screen	87.99	85.87	86.92
	Conversational	85.62	96.91	90.92
	Synthetic	98.09	97.53	97.81
MDMR	Screen	86.85	80.20	83.39
	Conversational	84.70	95.66	89.85
	Synthetic	97.92	97.21	97.56
QR	AER	92.48	90.42	91.44
	CbR	93.31	83.48	88.12

Table 4: Precision, recall and F1 scores for the MD, MR and QR models.

highlights the model's ability to carry over essential information through rewriting. In case of MR, we consider the ground truth mentions and compute the metrics by comparing the predicted entities with the true target entities. For MDMR, we use the predicted mentioned from MD to run MR, and then compute metrics by comparing all the predicted entities with the true entities.

Towards Harmful Erotic Content Detection through Coreference-Driven Contextual Analysis

WARNING: This paper contains material of a sensitive nature.

Inez Okulska and **Emilia Wiśnios**
{inez.okulska,emilia.wisnios}@nask.pl
NASK National Research Institute

Abstract

Adult content detection still poses a great challenge for automation. Existing classifiers primarily focus on distinguishing between erotic and non-erotic texts. However, they often need more nuance in assessing the potential harm. Unfortunately, the content of this nature falls beyond the reach of generative models due to its potentially harmful nature. Ethical restrictions prohibit large language models (LLMs) from analyzing and classifying harmful erotics, let alone generating them to create synthetic datasets for other neural models. In such instances where data is scarce and challenging, a thorough analysis of the structure of such texts rather than a large model may offer a viable solution. Especially given that harmful erotic narratives, despite appearing similar to harmless ones, usually reveal their harmful nature first through contextual information hidden in the non-sexual parts of the narrative.

This paper introduces a hybrid neural and rule-based context-aware system that leverages coreference resolution to identify harmful contextual cues in erotic content. Collaborating with professional moderators, we compiled a dataset and developed a classifier capable of distinguishing harmful from non-harmful erotic content. Our hybrid model, tested on Polish text, demonstrates a promising accuracy of 84% and a recall of 80%. Models based on RoBERTa and Longformer without explicit usage of coreference chains achieved significantly weaker results, underscoring the importance of coreference resolution in detecting such nuanced content as harmful erotics. This approach also offers the potential for enhanced visual explainability, supporting moderators in evaluating predictions and taking necessary actions to address harmful content.

1 Introduction

The identification of harmful content represents a fundamental application of Natural Language Processing (NLP) methods on the internet. Such harmful content encompasses various forms, including hate speech, offensive material, misinformation, and graphic content. Among these, harmful erotic narratives present a particularly sensitive challenge. However, **general adult content detection models primarily focus on distinguishing between non-erotic and erotic texts without nuances in terms of their potential harm**. This is particularly challenging given that the parts describing sexual encounters often appear quite similar in most narratives. **It is the contextual information and additional details describing the individuals involved in or subjected to these sexual actions that ultimately reveal their harmful nature**.

The sentence *"He made love with her"* is a common example of an sexual-related sentence that falls under adult content classification but is generally harmless. However, if the model can detect that elsewhere in the text, at some distance, there is a hint that the term *'her'* refers to a minor or a sibling, it can then raise awareness among readers or, even better, alert moderators to the potentially harmful nature of the text. **And that distant reference, that subtle hint, is precisely what coreference resolution is designed for – to comprehend the semantic chains throughout the narrative**.

In collaboration with moderators from an institution serving as part of a national Incidence Response Team, our research identified a gray area of harmful erotic content that could gain from a coreference-driven contextual analysis. While not yet illegal in certain jurisdictions, this content has the potential to inflict significant harm, particularly on younger or more vulnerable readers.

In this paper, we propose a hybrid context-aware system, using neural and rule-based components, for harmful content detection. It utilizes the coreference module for Polish spaCy model (Tuora and Kobylinski, 2019) to find interrelations between potentially hamrful contextual cues and sex-related parts. While several erotic content classifiers al-

Proceedings of the Sixth Workshop on Computational Models of Reference, Anaphora and Coreference (CRAC 2023), pages 59–70
December 6–7, 2023

ready exist, there is a conspicuous absence of harmful erotic content classifiers, particularly in languages like Polish. Although our proposed approach has been tested on Polish text, it can readily adapt to other languages, given the availability of BERT-based models and coreference resolution tools for those languages (which is the case for example for the English language).

The primary challenge in developing such a classifier is the scarcity of data. As this form of narrative content straddles the line between illegality and deviance, sourcing and collecting suitable training data poses a formidable obstacle. Unfortunately, the content of this nature falls beyond the reach of generative models due to its potentially harmful nature. **Ethical restrictions prohibit large language models (LLMs) from analyzing and classifying harmful erotics, let alone generating them to create synthetic datasets for other neural models**.

In our research, we assembled, together with the professional moderators, a modest dataset of 164 text samples, meticulously curated and flagged by them. While this dataset remains insufficient for training a robust classifier, it has proven adequate for extracting the harmful contextual features for the hybrid content classifier.

As a result, **we introduce a hybrid model capable of distinguishing between non-harmful and harmful erotic content by leveraging both sexual content predictions and contextual cues**. Our experiments, using real-life examples assessed by professional moderators, demonstrate the promise of this approach, achieving an accuracy of 84% and a recall of 80%. Furthermore, the model's high potential for explainability, thanks to its hybrid coreference-driven architecture, holds great significance for human moderators. They require this level of understanding to evaluate each prediction, make informed decisions, and ultimately classify the text, potentially taking actions such as removing the content from the web or contacting the authorities.

2 Related Work

The task of coreference resolution for the Polish language has been gaining attention for many years (Ogrodniczuk et al., 2014; Nitoń et al., 2018). In 2022, it was also one the subjects of the Shared Task at CRAC 2022 (Saputa, 2022a). There are free coreference tools available – a rule-based and a statistical resolution tool[1]. Both utilizing the Polish Coreference Corpus (Ogrodniczuk et al., 2016). Applications to which coreference resolution in Polish has been applied include document summarization (Kopeć, 2019) and information extraction (Kaczmarek and Marcińczuk, 2015). In the German language, it has been used for drama analysis (Pagel and Reiter, 2020), and in English, for the analysis of medical interviews (Uzuner et al., 2012).

The issue of gender bias in the Polish language concerning the detection of coreference chains was also studied (Zhu et al., 2016; Zhao et al., 2018; Kocmi et al., 2020)).

As for the detection of harmful content, the harmfulness of which becomes evident only in the context of the interrelationships between mentions, has not been the subject of research so far. This applies primarily to the Polish language, but also, to the best of our knowledge, to other languages.

Efforts in the field of automated Child Sexual Abuse Material (CSAM) detection have predominantly focused on identifying harmful images and videos (Lee et al., 2020). The use of actual CSAM material for model training is constrained by significant legal and ethical complexities. Consequently, researchers have explored alternative approaches, with an emphasis on metadata and filename detection (Pereira et al., 2021).

While textual CSAM content has garnered relatively less attention, Natural Language Processing (NLP) methods and stylometric techniques, such as author profiling, have been adapted for online child grooming detection (Borj et al., 2023). Emil Fleron, utilizing a dataset of abuse forum connections from the 2017 Freedom Hosting 2 dark net leak, investigated how supervised machine learning, relying solely on text data, can identify posts linked to CSAM distribution (Fleron, 2018). Text mining techniques have also been applied to the examination of medical documentation related to child abuse in the Netherlands (Amrit et al., 2017). In a different context, NLP-based methods have been employed to detect sexual/erotic content in user-generated online texts, aimed at filtering out content inappropriate for minors (Barrientos et al., 2020).

Recent studies have ventured into sentence-level pornographic content detection in Chinese and En-

[1]`http://zil.ipipan.waw.pl/PolishCoreferenceTools`

glish datasets comprising novels and stories (Song et al., 2021). However, these approaches are primarily designed to identify adult content, often neglecting the consideration of its harmful or non-harmful nature, and notably, none of them incorporate methods using coreference resolution.

In conclusion, the automated detection of harmful erotic narratives requires further development and investigation, and the incorporation of a coreference-based method represents a novel contribution to this field.

3 Data Collection and Preprocessing

Our hybrid coreference-driven model for harmful erotic content detection relies on two distinct datasets to facilitate and evaluate its functioning in Polish language: a set of sentences describing sexual encounters, called Sexual Sentences Dataset, and the collection of actual harmful erotic narratives, called Harmful Erotic Full-Text Dataset.

3.1 Sexual Sentences Dataset

The dataset comprises approximately 28000 sentences tokenized with NLTK library and selected for binary classification of sexual content with 5865 for class neutral and 22135 for sexual. We intentionally sampled and shuffled these sentences to obscure any contextual cues between adjacent sentences. This deliberate choice prevents the leakage of contextual information from one sentence to the next. For instance, consider the pair of sentences: "He touched her naked skin in a very intimate way. He could see that she loved it." When presented in an unshuffled narrative, the second sentence often led to false positive label 'sexual' due to prior knowledge, although it does not indicate any sexual activity itself. However, by annotating each sentence individually, such ambiguities were minimized.

Each sentence underwent manual labeling by three human annotators, final label was assigned as a result of majority voting. The percentage agreement was 87%. More details regarding annotation process is presented in the Appendix A.

These sentences were sourced from both non-professional and professional narratives gathered from a diverse array of online sources. These sources included web services specializing in short stories contributed by various authors, spanning categories such as "love," "life," "friendship," and "erotic." We did not perform any additional text preprocessing.

3.2 Harmful Erotic Full-Text Dataset

The second dataset served for the main task of the general detection of harmful erotic narratives, and has been split into training, test and validation set. The first one – encompassing 308 samples, has been used for analysis of coreference structures emerging in this type of narrative texts. The same dataset was used for training baseline models (see Section 7). The test set made of 78 samples was used for evaluating the performance of baseline models (Appendix C). The experiments proving the performance of the presented method in numbers, have been run on 164 previously unseen samples.

The harmful class within this dataset comprises text content collected by automated scrapers commissioned by a legal institution tasked with addressing cyber incidents of this nature. Manual classification of these texts was carried out by professionally trained moderators as part of their daily responsibilities.

In the beginning, the full-text corpus exclusively comprised non-professional narratives categorized by moderators under the CSAM (Child Sexual Abuse Material) classification. However, as we collaborated on developing automated classification algorithms, we identified a 'gray zone' of texts. These texts initially fell outside the strict confines of the CSAM definition but were nonetheless deemed disturbing and deviant by both professional and non-professional annotators, including members of the machine learning team.

As a result, we made the decision to expand the category beyond CSAM to encompass harmful-erotic content. This broader category includes all samples describing sexual relations involving young individuals marked by significant age and authority differentials, such as teacher-student dynamics, as well as various forms of incestuous narratives. This expansion specifically encompasses narratives where the focus lies on the sexual excitement induced by family relationships and/or the innocence of a young person, even extending to scenarios involving cousins.

The gathered text samples were tokenized using the same SpaCy model that was employed during the training of the binary sexual sentence classifier. No additional preprocessing steps were applied either before or after tokenization, ensuring the classifier's robustness in handling the natural online presence of such content.

4 RoBERTa-Based Sexual Sentence Classifier

The neural part of our hybrid approach relies on the sentence-level sexual sentence transformer classifier. It consists of RoBERTa base[2] and additional linear layers with dropout and ReLU activation build on top of the RoBERTa hidden state. The final version utilizes only the base version of the model, as our initial experiments have shown that bigger model does not improve the classification results significantly.

The Sexual Sentence Dataset (as described in Section 3.1) was divided into train (22400) and test (5600) with similar distributions of the classes in both datasets, being approximately 3:1 (non-sexual:sexual).

In its final architecture the model utilizes three linear layers were (with sizes: 768, 512, 256, 1). Dropout probability was equal 0.2. The model was trained on 5 epochs (effect of early stopping based on the validation loss), using Adam as the optimizer with the learning rate of 1e-5. Table 1 shows the results.

Table 1: Classification Report for validation set. "Prec." = precision, "Rec." = recall, "Sup" = support.

	Prec.	**Rec.**	**F1**	**Sup.**
Non-Sexual	0.96	0.96	0.96	4427
Sexual	0.84	0.83	0.84	1173
Accuracy			0.93	5600
Macro avg	0.90	0.89	0.90	5600
Weighted avg	0.93	0.93	0.93	5600

5 Coreference Resolution for Contextual Analysis

Our choice of the coreference resolution method is driven by the recognition that it is the context or scene within these narratives that typically distinguishes harmless erotica from potentially harmful variants. Detailed descriptions of the actors or objects involved in the sexual actions often reside in separate sentences from those describing the actions themselves. The presented method combines information from sentences classified as sexual, i.e., those describing sexual activities, with contextual information linked to individuals mentioned in these sentences through a coreference chain as shown in the Algorithm 1. We have decided to use a coreference model for the Polish language proposed by Saputa (2022b), based on the HerBERT model (Mroczkowski et al., 2021). This is an end-to-end model, conveniently integrated into the Polish spaCy model, that achieved an F1 score of 76.67 in the CRAC Shared Task 2022 (Žabokrtský and Ogrodniczuk, 2022) on the Polish test dataset.

First, each sentence receives prediction regarding whether they contain sexual content or not. For the list of all sexual sentences, position indices in the document are determined, ranging from the first to the last token for each sexual sentence. Subsequently, all detected coreference chains in the text are examined to determine if they contain significant contextual information based on the contextual features described in Section 6. If such elements are identified, mention positions are established and compared with the index ranges for the sexual sentences. This process checks whether a given potentially harmful cue refers to another word that is part of a sentence describing sexual activity. Grammatical dependencies are also examined concerning the verbal phrases in the sexual sentence.

Contextual elements in such chains can contain information directly — the same or synonymous noun forms, personal pronouns, or possessives. A crucial aspect of this analysis is the syntactic relationship, which allows us to determine whether, in the case of multiple references to individuals, they are indeed participating in the activities described in the sexual sentence.

Figure 1 illustrates how contextual cues are distributed, and how the coreference mechanism allows for their identification, thereby distinguishing harmful from non-harmful erotic content, as well as shows the visualization potential of this approach. The provided example describes an erotic situation. The text highlighted in red has received a "sexual" label from the binary neural model because it describes sexual activities. However, these words are inherently neutral:

'Wtedy on wsadził mi rękę pod bluzkę dotykając moich piersi, nachylił się całując me usta' ('Then he slid his hand under my shirt, touching my breasts, leaned in to kiss my lips').

However, thanks to coreference resolution, it be-

[2] https://huggingface.co/sdadas/polish-roberta-base-v2

Algorithm 1 Coreference resolution between harmful contextual features and sex-related sentences

```
Requires:
    doc                 The SpaCy Doc type
    sentences           List of input sentences
    coref_chains        List of doc coreference chains
    harm_context_feats  List of contextual features
                        (creating harmful context)
    seuxal_model        RoBERTa-based sexual sentence
                        classifier
sexual_ids ← [ ]
for sentence ∈ sentences do
    sexual_content ← SEXUAL_MODEL(sentence)
    sexual_sent_id ← SENTENCE POSITION IN DOC
    if sexual_content >= 0.5 then
        sexual_ids.APPEND(sexual_sent_id)

harm_context_clusters ← [ ]
for chain ∈ coref_chains do
    chain_ids ← ALL DOC POSITIONS IN CHAIN
    for mention ∈ chain do
        if mention ∈ harm_context_feats then
            harm_context_ids.APPEND(chain_ids)
        if harm_context_ids ∈ sexual_ids then
            harm_context_clusters.APPEND(chain)
    if harm_context_clusters then
        label = harmful
    else
        label = non-harmful
return label
```

comes evident that the *'he'* in the sexual sentence is part of a longer chain, which allows us to decipher that it refers to a "guardian" and simultaneously a "P.E. teacher," indicating a physical education teacher.

On its own, the word *'nauczyciel'* ('teacher') can merely serve as a hint about the profession, which is still insufficient to unequivocally classify the content as harmful. However, the second chain leaves no doubt. The analysis of the syntactic dependency in the highlighted sexual sentence demonstrates that the person who is subjected to the sexual activity 'Wtedy on wsadził *mi* rękę pod bluzkę' ('he slipped his hand under *my* shirt') is linked in a single chain with the descriptions '*my* guardian' and '*my* P.E. teacher,' unequivocally suggesting that this person is a student and we are dealing with a harmful sexual relationship between a school teacher and his female student.

Additionally, context elements related to the actors participating in sexual sentences but not directly describing the actors themselves, such as elements of their clothing or body parts, were examined. As described in Section 6, the analysis of the training set revealed the unique presence of certain terms. Therefore, we decided to include them in the set of potentially harmful contextual clues that are detected in the coreference chain encompassing a sexual sentence.

This also applies to various variations of age representation, where the presence of age-related terms was, as in other cases, linked through syntactic dependencies. If a sexual sentence contains subject or object descriptors of sexual activities that, through coreference chains, connect with another sentence containing age-related terms referring to the same person it is a clear indicator for the text label to be 'harmful'. For example, in the sexual sentence *'He touched me'* and the *'me'* connects with *'I'* in another sentence, which is the subject of *'I was 15 years old'*.

6 Contextual Features for Harmful Erotic Content Detection

The coreference features have been automatically extracted and subjected to domain expert analysis. These features form the basis for the rule-based component of the hybrid model and allow for identifying specific elements of context relevant to the analysis of coreference chains related to the sentences describing sexual activities.

From the training set, all text samples involving sexual actions were selected, leaving two classes – of harmful and non-harmful erotic narratives. The TF-IDF analysis was conducted on both of them separately, and based on it, the most frequently occurring words in their base forms (lemmas) were selected for each class. Only those belonging to the category 'noun' (part of speech) were filtered out from them. Then, among them, only those belonging to the 'person' semantic category were chosen, as the most crucial distinguishing element between non-harmful and harmful erotica is the set of actors participating in or being subject to sexual activities. This list ultimately includes 103 nouns.

One of the most striking examples of differences is the word *'mama'* ('mother'), which appeared 303 times in harmful erotica and only four times in the non-harmful class, and *'syn'* ('son'), which appeared 151 times in harmful erotica and 0 times in the non-harmful class. This set of features mainly includes family members, teachers, and terms for children and young people in official, colloquial, and containing typical spelling errors.

Additionally, analyses of both lexicon distributions showed significant differences in the occurrence of additional elements describing scenery –

Mój wfista patrzał na mnie z niezbyt dobrą miną.. nie zwracałam na niego uwagi, zaczęłam ćwiczyć jak inni. Po lekcji mieliśmy pięć minut przerwy, wtedy nic szczególnego się nie działo. Po dzwonku na kolejny wf znów mieliśmy wyjść na salę, ale mój wychowawca mnie zatrzymał (mieliśmy łączone z drugą klasą więc jego obowiązki przejął drugi nauczyciel), kazał mi iść za nim do pokoju nauczycielskiego.
Gdy już weszliśmy, zaczęło się..
- Dlaczego znów się spóźniłaś, Paulinko?
Ja: Zaspałam..
- Kolejny raz? Wiesz, że jak tak dalej pójdzie to nie dam Ci nawet dwójki z powodu Twoich nieobecności. (...)
Powiedział po czym wstał z krzesła i udał się do drzwi, poszłam za nim kiedy on zamknął je na klucz i odwrócił się.. zesztywniałam. Zbliżył się i popchnął mnie na ścianę.. nie wiedziałam co powiedzieć, wyszeptałam tylko 'nie chcę'.
Wtedy on wsadził mi rękę pod bluzkę dotykając moich piersi, nachylił się całując me usta.

Figure 1: Example of visualization the contextual clues through coreference resolution. Marker colors: 1) red - sentence classified as sexual, 2) yellow - one coreference chain referring to the male person involved in the sexual action, 3) green - coreference chain referring to the subject of the sexual action.

parts of clothing and body parts. In the case of the CSAM class, there was an overrepresentation of female clothing elements in the diminutive form (*'spódniczka'*, 'little skirt', *'staniczek'*, *'camisole')*, also in a characteristic form of non-professional, affective writing, which is not subject to editing, with spelling errors. Importantly, misspelled words do not undergo automatic lemmatization, so it was essential to include them in their original form, e.g.,: *'soudniczke', 'sludniczke', 'spudnice', 'spudnicze', 'spudniczkach', 'spudniczki'* (there are all misspelled version of the word 'little skirt')

Words describing genitalia, characteristic of the harmful class (and not present in the non-harmful class), are vulgar forms that have undergone morphological diminution. On one hand, there is an "adult" term for intimate body parts suitable for sexual actions. On the other hand, there is some adjustment to underage participants (not suitable for sexual actions!) by using diminutive forms. Such a form (e.g., *'kutasik'*, 'tiny little cock') is not encountered either in reference to adults (in that case, the diminutive would imply at least a derogatory, mocking attitude toward the described body part) or in neutral anatomical descriptions of children, where vulgar synonyms for official terms are not used, at most endearing ones (*'siusiak'*,'wee-wee').

As a result of the analysis of extracted nouns, it also turned out to be worthwhile to introduce a negative rule weakening the probability of prediction for the harmful erotic class based on words characteristic only for non-harmful erotica. In the harmful class, the words *'mąż'* ('husband') and *'żona'* ('wife') did not appear once (only one occurrence of *'żoneczka'*, 'wifey'). In contrast, in the non-harmful erotic class, *'żona'* and *'mąż'* appear pretty often, 113 and 71, respectively.

Additional features detected in the text relate to age and include numerical, verbal, and verbal-numerical representations, taking into account typical forms of misspelling in terms of punctuation and spelling. The upper age limit, which is flagged, is 17 years.

7 Experiments and Results

Detailed description of used RoBERTa model for sentence classification (first step of our classifier to identify sexual vs non-sexual content) is presented in Section 6. As for the full classification, the results were tested on independent real-life data, which consisted of 34 harmful stories and 130 non-harmful stories.

For the full-text classification of harmful erotic content, we compared our proposed coreference-driven approach with RoBERTa base model[3] trained for 10 and for 20 epochs, the Longformer base[4], and a baseline model. Similar to our proposed model, this baseline relies first on identifying sexual sentences with fine-tuned RoBERTa and then is looking for phrases suggesting harmful

[3] https://huggingface.co/sdadas/polish-roberta-base-v2

[4] https://huggingface.co/sdadas/polish-longformer-base-4096

Table 2: Results from evaluation of all models on the test dataset made from 164 stories unseed in the training and validation phase. Details regarding parameters used for RoBERTa model and Longformer model are available in Appendix C.

Model	Recall	Precision	F1	Accuracy
RoBERTa base fine-tuned for 10 epoch	91%	30%	63%	45%
RoBERTa base fine-tuned for 20 epoch	70,5%	65%	68%	88%
Longformer	82%	49%	61%	81%
Coreference-Driven Hybrid Classifier	**80%**	**70,5%**	**75%**	**84%**
Baseline Classifier (without coreference resolution)	14%	100%	24%	77,5%

context (both the baseline and coreference-driven model utilize the same dictionaries and semantic rules as described in Section 6). However, the main difference is that the baseline searches for these phrases exclusively in those sentences that have been identified (predicted) as sexual. In contrast, the coreference-driven model seeks contexts in sentences that are not necessary sexual per se (predicted in the first step as "neutral") but connected to sexual ones through the coreference chains. The results of both models demonstrate that the difference in searching for cues in a direct (without utilizing the coreference chains) and a broader context (with coreference chains) is crucial for capturing harmful content.

As shown in Table 2, the RoBERTa base trained for ten epochs seems to be the best in the hunt for the harmful erotica with its 91% recall. However, its focus on the harmful class let the precision drop to a disturbing rate of 30%, meaning that 70% of all non-harmful erotic stories would have been accused of containing some sort of deviation. The analogous issue can be observed in the case of the Langformer model, which offers high recall (82%) but still a very low precision (49%)).

Thus, for the task of detecting harmful erotica the combination of recall, accuracy, and F1-Score is crucial for evaluating such a model instead of solely focusing on the highest recall. Detecting harmful content is a delicate matter since classifying a text with the "harmful" label may even cause legal actions. Therefore, leveraging high recall with high precision is significant in this case. Longer training of RoBERTa improved the precision significantly, but the recall fell by over 20 percentage points, which shows that this architecture cannot find the right balance for this case.

As already mentioned, one of the main challenges for detecting harmful erotic narratives is the collection of the training dataset. Most probably, the Longformer or the RoBERTa model could have shown more potential when presented with more training data. However, in this real-world case, it was necessary to find a working solution to overcome the problem of such a scarce dataset that was only possible to gather. Also given the fact that this kind of data cannot be effectively generated to enhance the dataset synthetically.

The coreference-driven model achieves a satisfying recall (of 80%) and accuracy (84%), together with good precision and the best F1-Score (75%). As the results show, the coreference-driven rules enhancing the neural sexual sentence classifier offer very promising alternative to the end-to-end models when the training data is lacking.

The results of full-text classification for the coreference-driven classifier are clearly dependent on the performance of the sexual sentence classifier. **Manual analysis of both false negatives and false positives of the coreference-driven hybrid model reveals that the majority of errors stem from an excessive or inaccurate classification of sentences as sexual.** Only in four cases of false negative, despite the accurate classification of sexual sentences, the syntactic relationships in the text proved to be too complex to unequivocally trace the connections between harmful contextual elements and the sexual actions and correctly label the text as harmful. This led us to believe that the proposed approach is perfectly worthy of consideration and further development, mainly focused on improvements of the RoBERTa-based sexual sentence classifier.

8 Discussion

The main challenge in detecting harmful erotica lies in the fact that **merely identifying sexual sentences is insufficient. What makes a text genuinely harmful often requires a comprehensive reading to extract the information from a**

complex context, including entirely non-sexual sentences. This is why the baseline model that searched for the contextual clues only in the direct sexual sentences failed significantly (with the recall of 14%) in the overall detection of harmful content: the clues are usually located outside the sexual sentences. However, previous experiments have also shown that a simple full-text search for the clues (the keyphrases related to age, occupation, or family relationships) is also not enough. That is because these terms can appear in the text, but in a completely neutral context of world-building, unrelated to the sexual activity itself, an innocent part of the depicted world. **Hence, it is only through analysis using coreference resolution that we can search for and determine the true nature of the contextual clues and their relationships to the sexual content.**

9 Limitations and Future Work

Insufficient Harmful Data Availability. A notable limitation of this study lies in the limited availability of harmful data for thorough analysis. The acquisition and accessibility of datasets containing instances of harmful activities have posed significant challenges. To address this limitation, we intend to expand our data collection efforts in future research endeavors. Increasing the volume of available data is vital for enhancing the comprehensiveness and robustness of our analysis and findings.

The model for sexual sentence classification is far from perfect yet. An essential component of the presented algorithm, despite the critical role of coreference, is the detection of sexual sentences within the text. If the model's prediction is incorrect, it can have a negative impact on the overall assessment of the text as harmful because each coreference chain is invariably linked to sentences classified as sexual. In the subsequent stages of the project, we plan to gather and annotate a more diverse set of data and then improve the quality of this classifier.

Adoption of a Learning-Based Approach Over Rule-Based. The current contextual features were manually selected based on tf-idf analysis. With a larger corpus of available texts, it would be feasible to train a dedicated model capable of automatically detecting the presence of these features within the text. This shift toward a learning-based approach would enhance the system's adaptability and performance, as it could better capture intricate patterns and nuances within the data.

10 Conclusion

Addressing the demanding yet significant application of coreference resolution to harmful erotic content detection, we offer the following contributions:

1. A first neural model fine-tuned solely for classifying sexual sentences in the Polish language, based on the RoBERTa model and trained on 28000 manually annotated sentences.

2. A hybrid neural and rule-based model for detecting harmful erotic content, which leverages coreference resolution to extract necessary contextual clues. This way, it is capable of effectively distinguishing non-harmful from harmful erotic narratives.

3. A visual explanation method for the model potentially highly beneficial for professional moderators involved in the detection of such texts in their work.

4. Preliminary analysis of the issue of harmful erotica in the Polish language.

Acknowledgments

The results presented in this paper are a culmination of the research conducted as part of the project titled "APAKT – A system responding to child safety threats in cyberspace with special emphasis on child pornography", generously funded by the National Center for Research and Development (NCBR) within the initiative CYBERSECIDENT/455132/III/NCBR/2020.

We extend our heartfelt thanks to the team of moderators from 'Dyżurnet' who provided invaluable assistance throughout the research process.

References

Chintan Amrit, Tim Paauw, Robin Aly, and Miha Lavric. 2017. Identifying child abuse through text mining and machine learning. *Expert systems with applications*, 88:402–418.

Gonzalo Molpeceres Barrientos, Rocío Alaíz-Rodríguez, Víctor González-Castro, and Andrew C. Parnell. 2020. Machine learning techniques for the detection of inappropriate erotic content in text. *Int. J. Comput. Intell. Syst.*, 13(1):591–603.

Parisa Rezaee Borj, Kiran B. Raja, and Patrick Bours. 2023. Online grooming detection: A comprehensive survey of child exploitation in chat logs. *Knowl. Based Syst.*, 259:110039.

Emil Fleron. 2018. Automatic classification of text regarding child sexual abusive material.

Adam Kaczmarek and Michał Marcińczuk. 2015. Evaluation of coreference resolution tools for polish from the information extraction perspective. In *The 5th Workshop on Balto-Slavic Natural Language Processing*, pages 24–33.

Tom Kocmi, Tomasz Limisiewicz, and Gabriel Stanovsky. 2020. Gender coreference and bias evaluation at wmt 2020. *arXiv preprint arXiv:2010.06018*.

Mateusz Kopeć. 2019. Three-step coreference-based summarizer for polish news texts. *Poznan Studies in Contemporary Linguistics*, 55(2):397–443.

Hee-Eun Lee, Tatiana Ermakova, Vasilis Ververis, and Benjamin Fabian. 2020. Detecting child sexual abuse material: A comprehensive survey. *Forensic Science International: Digital Investigation*, 34:301022.

Robert Mroczkowski, Piotr Rybak, Alina Wróblewska, and Ireneusz Gawlik. 2021. HerBERT: Efficiently pretrained transformer-based language model for Polish. In *Proceedings of the 8th Workshop on Balto-Slavic Natural Language Processing*, pages 1–10, Kiyv, Ukraine. Association for Computational Linguistics.

Bartłomiej Nitoń, Paweł Morawiecki, and Maciej Ogrodniczuk. 2018. Deep neural networks for coreference resolution for polish. In *Proceedings of the Eleventh International Conference on Language Resources and Evaluation (LREC 2018)*.

Maciej Ogrodniczuk, Katarzyna Glowinska, Mateusz Kopec, Agata Savary, and Magdalena Zawislawska. 2014. *Coreference: annotation, resolution and evaluation in Polish*. Walter de Gruyter GmbH & Co KG.

Maciej Ogrodniczuk, Katarzyna Głowińska, Mateusz Kopeć, Agata Savary, and Magdalena Zawisławska. 2016. Polish coreference corpus. In *Human Language Technology. Challenges for Computer Science and Linguistics: 6th Language and Technology Conference, LTC 2013, Poznań, Poland, December 7-9, 2013. Revised Selected Papers 6*, pages 215–226. Springer.

Janis Pagel and Nils Reiter. 2020. Gerdracor-coref: A coreference corpus for dramatic texts in german. In *Proceedings of the Twelfth Language Resources and Evaluation Conference*, pages 55–64.

Mayana Pereira, Rahul Dodhia, Hyrum Anderson, and Richard Brown. 2021. Metadata-based detection of child sexual abuse material.

Karol Saputa. 2022a. Coreference resolution for polish: Improvements within the crac 2022 shared task. In *Proceedings of the CRAC 2022 Shared Task on Multilingual Coreference Resolution*, pages 18–22.

Karol Saputa. 2022b. Coreference resolution for Polish: Improvements within the CRAC 2022 shared task. In *Proceedings of the CRAC 2022 Shared Task on Multilingual Coreference Resolution*, pages 18–22, Gyeongju, Republic of Korea. Association for Computational Linguistics.

Kaisong Song, Yangyang Kang, Wei Gao, Zhe Gao, Changlong Sun, and Xiaozhong Liu. 2021. Evidence aware neural pornographic text identification for child protection. In *Thirty-Fifth AAAI Conference on Artificial Intelligence, AAAI 2021, Thirty-Third Conference on Innovative Applications of Artificial Intelligence, IAAI 2021, The Eleventh Symposium on Educational Advances in Artificial Intelligence, EAAI 2021, Virtual Event, February 2-9, 2021*, pages 14939–14947. AAAI Press.

Ryszard Tuora and Łukasz Kobylinski. 2019. Integrating polish language tools and resources in spacy. In *Proceedings of PP-RAI 2019 Conference*, pages 210–214.

Ozlem Uzuner, Andreea Bodnari, Shuying Shen, Tyler Forbush, John Pestian, and Brett R South. 2012. Evaluating the state of the art in coreference resolution for electronic medical records. *Journal of the American Medical Informatics Association*, 19(5):786–791.

Zdeněk Žabokrtský and Maciej Ogrodniczuk, editors. 2022. *Proceedings of the CRAC 2022 Shared Task on Multilingual Coreference Resolution*. Association for Computational Linguistics, Gyeongju, Republic of Korea.

Jieyu Zhao, Tianlu Wang, Mark Yatskar, Vicente Ordonez, and Kai-Wei Chang. 2018. Gender bias in coreference resolution: Evaluation and debiasing methods. *arXiv preprint arXiv:1804.06876*.

Rui Zhu, Krzysztof Janowicz, Bo Yan, and Yingjie Hu. 2016. Which kobani? a case study on the role of spatial statistics and semantics for coreference resolution across gazetteers. In *International conference on GIScience short paper proceedings*, volume 1.

A Annotation Details

In this section, we provide a comprehensive account of the annotation process, including the guidelines used, for classifying sentences as either sexual (1) or non-sexual (0) within the scope of our study. To minimize the potential influence of context, the sentences for annotation were intentionally shuffled. The process involved the participation of three annotators for each sentence, with the final label determined through a majority voting mechanism.

A.1 Annotation Process

Annotators. Three human annotators were engaged for the task of sentence classification, each chosen for their proficiency in the target language and their prior experience with similar annotation tasks. These annotators were selected based on their ability to adhere to the annotation guidelines and their capacity to independently assess the sentences.

Majority Voting. To maintain the robustness and objectivity of the annotation process, we employed a majority voting system. For each shuffled sentence, the three annotators independently assigned a label (1 for sexual or 0 for non-sexual). The final label for each sentence was determined through a majority vote. In instances of a tie, a consensus was reached through discussion among the annotators.

A.2 Annotation Guidelines.

Comprehensive and well-defined annotation guidelines were crucial to achieving consistency and accuracy in the annotation process. The following summarizes the key aspects of the annotation guidelines:

Sexual Sentence Definition. A sexual sentence, as stipulated for this annotation task, is one that includes explicit content related to sexual activities or themes. Sentences depicting ordinary acts of affection such as kissing, holding hands, or hugging should not be classified as sexual. Annotators were instructed to focus on the presence of explicit or graphic language, descriptions of sexual acts, or content intended to discuss or explore sexual arousal as indicative of a sexual sentence.

Ambiguity and Context Independence. Given that sentences were presented without context, annotators were instructed to assess each sentence independently. Ambiguity in the sexual nature of a sentence should be resolved based on the sentence's content alone. Annotators should not make assumptions or rely on contextual information that is not explicitly provided.

Consistency and Objectivity. Annotators were encouraged to maintain a consistent approach throughout the annotation process and to avoid the introduction of personal biases. Classification should be solely based on the content of the sentence and its alignment with the provided definition of a sexual sentence.

Annotator Discussions. In cases of uncertainty or disagreement among annotators, open discussions were encouraged to facilitate consensus and ensure the accuracy of the final label. Annotators were allowed to consult relevant reference materials or seek clarification from the research team to address any doubts.

A.3 Inter-Annotator Agreement

To evaluate the reliability of the annotation process, inter-annotator agreement scores were calculated. These scores provide insights into the consistency among annotators and the overall quality of the annotations, considering that sentences were presented without contextual information. We assessed inter-annotator agreement using three commonly employed metrics: Fleiss' Kappa, Cohen's Kappa, and Percentage Agreement.

Fleiss' Kappa. Fleiss' Kappa is a measure of agreement between multiple annotators when categorizing items into multiple categories. For our task of classifying sentences as sexual (1) or non-sexual (0), Fleiss' Kappa was calculated as 0.79. This indicates substantial agreement among annotators.

Cohen's Kappa. Cohen's Kappa measures the agreement between two annotators. It was used to assess pairwise agreement among our annotators. The average Cohen's Kappa across all pairs of annotators was found to be 0.72, indicating substantial agreement between individual pairs.

Percentage Agreement. Percentage agreement, which measures the proportion of sentences for which all annotators agreed on the same label, was 87%.

A.4 Examples

To illustrate the nature of sentences classified as sexual or non-sexual, we provide the following examples from our dataset along with their corresponding annotations in the Table 6.

B Sources of data

All non-professional stories were scrapped from publicly available websites, including

- *opowiadaniaerotyczne-darmowo.com*
- *sexopowiadania.pl*
- *pornzone.com*

- *anonserek.pl*
- *opowi.pl* (categories: o życiu, różne, miłosne)
- *opowiadania.pl*
- *polki.pl*

We utilized maximum of 2 stories from the same author.

C Details regarding training parameters

In this section we present parameters used for training baselines models (Table 7) and classification reports on the baselines models (Tables 3, 4, 5).

Table 3: Classification Raport for validation set for baseline RoBERTa model trained on 10 epochs. Prec. means precision and Rec. means recall.

	Prec.	**Rec.**	**F1**	**Sup.**
Non-harmful	0.96	0.71	0.82	38
Harmful	0.78	0.97	0.87	40
Accuracy			0.85	78
Macro avg	0.87	0.84	0.84	78
Weighted avg	0.87	0.85	0.84	78

Table 4: Classification Raport for validation set for baseline RoBERTa model trained on 20 epochs. Prec. means precision and Rec. means recall.

	Prec.	**Rec.**	**F1**	**Sup.**
Non-harmful	0.75	1.0	0.85	38
Harmful	1.0	0.68	0.81	40
Accuracy			0.83	78
Macro avg	0.87	0.84	0.83	78
Weighted avg	0.88	0.83	0.83	78

Table 5: Classification Raport for validation set for baseline Longformer model. Prec. means precision and Rec. means recall.

	Prec.	**Rec.**	**F1**	**Sup.**
Non-harmful	0.82	0.89	0.85	35
Harmful	0.90	0.84	0.87	43
Accuracy			0.86	78
Macro avg	0.86	0.86	0.86	78
Weighted avg	0.86	0.86	0.86	78

Table 6: Examples of Sentence Classification with Sexual Content (A1 – Annotator 1, A2 - Annotator 2, A3 – Annotator 3) **Warning: This table contains sentences with sexual content. Reader discretion is strongly advised.**

Sentence	Translation	A1	A2	A3	Majority Label
Pocałunek trwał kilka sekund.	The kiss lasted for a few seconds.	0	0	0	0
Obciągnęłam spódnicę i cofnęłam nogę pod stół.	I pulled down my skirt and withdrew my leg under the table.	0	0	1	0
Marcin pomógł jej pozbyć się swoich spodni.	Marcin helped her get rid of her pants.	0	1	0	0
Robił to powoli, z czasem przyspieszył, a ja już nie mogłam.	He did it slowly, and over time he sped up, and I couldn't do it anymore.	0	1	1	1
Wstał, a ja uklęknęłam przed nim, wzięłam znowu do ust.	He stood up, and I knelt in front of him, took to my mouth again.	1	1	1	1
Po chwili przyciągnął Joannę do siebie.	After a while, he pulled Joanna close to him.	0	0	0	0

Table 7: Training parameters for baseline models

Parameter	RoBERTa based 10	RoBERTa base 20	Longformer
learning rate	$1e-5$	$1e-5$	$1e-5$
number of epochs	10	10	10
optimizer	Adam	Adam	Adam
batch size	8	8	8
number of linear layers	3	3	3
dropout probability	0.2	0.2	0.2
activation layer	ReLU	ReLU	ReLU

Integrated Annotation of Event Structure, Object States, and Entity Coreference

Kyeongmin Rim and **James Pustejovsky**
Department of Computer Science
Brandeis University
Waltham, Massachusetts
{krim,jamesp}@brandeis.edu

Abstract

Understanding coreference and anaphora is still considered as a hard problem for NLP applications. Recent studies on modeling and annotating coreference and/or anaphoric relations show that the problem is a hard problem even for human expert annotators. In this work, we demonstrate an annotation environment that enables quick and easy, but still flexible annotation of coreference relations based on event semantics and argument structure, and constraints arsing from temporal logic. The main focus of the environment is to integrate annotation of lexically anchored entity state change tracking and coreference chains along the event-based entity transformation. The scheme and environment is developed as open source, and is publicly available.

1 Introduction

Coreference is linguistic phenomenon in which two or more expressions refer to a single real-world entity. Understanding coreferent relations in documents and dialogue is important in natural language processing (NLP) systems because it allows not only understanding the meaning of language, but also re-grouping events and statements around different participating entities that can be used in automatic summarization, for example.

Although annotating coreference in textual data has been an active research topic for a long time, early compilations of large corpora for computational operationalization of coreference resolution, such as MUC (Grishman and Sundheim, 1996; Hirschman and Chinchor, 1998), ACE (Doddington et al., 2004), or OntoNotes (Hovy et al., 2006; Pradhan et al., 2011), were focused on developing straightforward schemes to recognize fully identical denotations of entity mentions, especially pronominal anaphora.

However, it is often difficult to strictly define "identity" relations between two referring expressions or the denotations of those expressions. For example, in procedural texts such as cooking recipes, when entities in the text undergo a series of events that cause changes in their state, it is often impossible to accurately link entity mentions in anaphoric and/or coreference relations without modeling the differences (*state-wise*) between the "same" (*substance-wise*) entity before and after the transformations caused by events.

For example, let's consider a recipe for a PB&J sandwich where the entity "peanut butter" is mentioned multiple times. The peanut butter that is mentioned at the beginning of the recipe is the same physical substance that is mentioned at the end of the recipe. However, they are not exactly the same in that the peanut butter at the beginning of the recipe is probably in a jar, while the peanut butter at the end of the recipe is spread on bread. To accurately link these two mentions of "peanut butter" as *coreferent*, we need to model the difference between the two states of the peanut butter.

This is just one example of how difficult it can be to define coreference relations based on binary identity/non-identity classification between two referring expressions. In general, it is a challenging task that requires careful consideration of the context in which the expressions are used and commonsense knowledge of object interactions.

In this work, we demonstrate an annotation environment that can integrate annotation of temporal ordering and dependency of events, event argument structures, and coreference relations with full- and near-identity.

2 Background

Many of early research effort on coreference and anaphora annotation has been centered around identifying full identity relations. However, this approach sometimes fails to provide a rigorous definition of the *sameness* (Poesio et al., 2006) or misses many other important types of coreference relations (Zeldes, 2022), such as when two referring

Proceedings of the Sixth Workshop on Computational Models of Reference, Anaphora and Coreference (CRAC 2023), pages 71–77
December 6–7, 2023

expressions refer to two different states of the same entity (Rim et al., 2023).

When it comes to technical aspects of annotating coreference, due to the highly complex nature of coreference and anaphoric relations and lack of complete one-key definition of those relations, the annotation is usually done by trained linguistic experts to create large-scale public datasets (Pradhan et al., 2012; Uryupina et al., 2016). Recently, more efforts on gamifying the coreference annotation (Chamberlain et al., 2016) or crowd-sourcing it (Gupta et al., 2023) were reported. Still, due to the fundamental complexity of the phenomena that often requires long-distance context and inevitable ambiguity by polysemous use of language, deconstructing coreference annotation tasks into crowd-friendly simple questions remains an unresolved problem. Because of reliance on highly trained expert annotators, many annotation environments specifically developed for coreference annotation are often designed to rely on heavy cognitive work of annotators. For instance, annotating coreference relations are frequently done (simultaneously with detecting entity mentions) as drawing *chains* of coreferences across different parts of a document. Thus, annotators are required to look at the entire document all the time jumping top to bottom, and use pointer devices to precisely drag-and-draw links that often graphically rendered as lines/arrows (Müller and Strube, 2006; Widlöcher and Mathet, 2012) or color-coded bag-of-mentions (Oberle, 2018; Reiter, 2018; Aralikatte and Søgaard, 2020).

More recently, identifying and modeling different types of coreference relations beyond full identity-based binary classification has been attracting more attention in the community (Recasens et al., 2010; Fang et al., 2022) These non-identity or near-identity coreference relations are often called *bridging* relations (Poesio and Artstein, 2008; Roesiger et al., 2018). More specifically, coreference study in procedural text is gaining more attention, based on corpus from cooking recipes or how-to domains (Mori et al., 2014; Prange et al., 2019; Fang et al., 2022).

Procedural texts are also a good source material for entity state tracking. This is because they often describe the steps involved in completing a task, which can be used to track the state of entities as they move through the process. Tracking the state of the entities in a procedural text is also

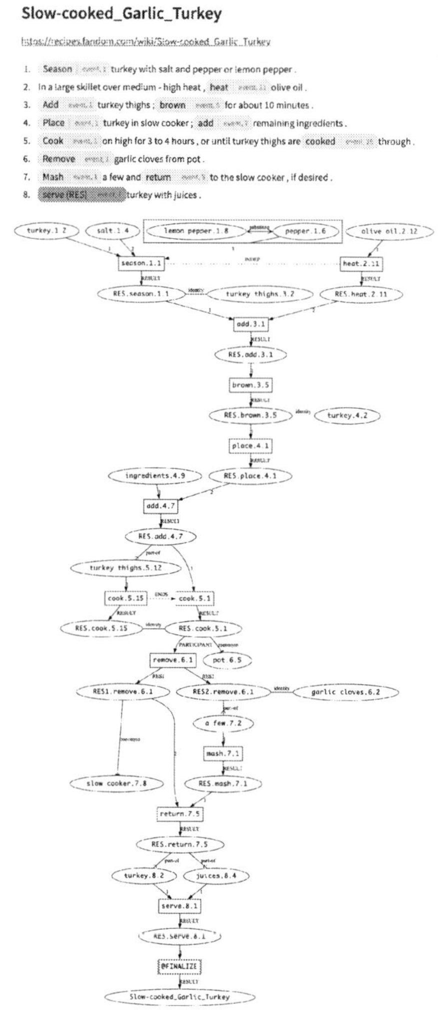

Figure 1: A full recipe text and its CUTL annotation in graph form, annotated using the new CUTLER. Rectangular nodes are events (processes) and oval nodes are entity mentions (inputs and outputs), indexed with token location. Then, coreference relations in solid edges, state changes in arrows, and event dependencies in dotted edges.

very important to understand the text and how the task is being completed. However, many studies on state change annotations have been too restrictive in terms of the state vocabulary to capture the full range of object transformations (Dalvi et al., 2018), or too open to the extent that some of the annotated data is totally unbound from any lexical clues (Tandon et al., 2020), that can cause a system based on such annotated training data to malfunction, such as hallucination in text generation (Wu et al., 2023).

3 Proposed Annotation scheme

In our previous work (Rim et al., 2023), we developed Coreference under Transformation Labeling (CUTL) annotation scheme and CUTLER[1], its paired integrated annotation environment, that enables annotation of event argument structures and coreference relations. In this work, we continue the work and propose a newer version that integrates temporal ordering of events and event dependencies in a multi-pass workflow. The annotation results are stored in graphs and thus, intermediate annotation progress can be easily visualized in real-time so that annotators can visually keep track of event-event relations (temporal order, conditional dependency), entity-event relations (argument structure), and entity-entity relations (different types of coreference relations). Our new contribution is expanding the previous work by adding annotation of event-event relations and flexibility in annotating sub-types of coreference relations.

3.1 Process-oriented event model and event dependency

The work is based on the process-oriented event model. The model is a way of representing an event as a transformation process that has inputs and outputs. Based on the model, all event mentions (verbs) create "phantom" result entities that can be used as regular entities for anchoring coreference link annotations in the rest of the timeline of the document. And the events themselves are used as a coreference relation to represent a type of near-identity between two nodes in the I/O graph. For example:

(1) a. **[Chop]**$_{res1}$ **[onion]**$_{ent1}$.
$ent1$: "(whole) `onion`"
$res1$: "(chopped onion)"
$ent1 \xleftrightarrow[\text{NEAR-IDENTITY}]{} res1$

b. **[Chop]**$_{res1}$ **[onion]**$_{ent1}$, and **[add]**$_{res2}$ **[onion]**$_{ent2}$ to the pan.
$ent1$: "(whole) `onion`"
$res1$: "(chopped onion)"
$ent2$: "(chopped) `onion`"
$ent1 \xleftrightarrow[\text{NEAR-IDENTITY}]{} res1$
$res1 \xleftrightarrow[\text{FULL-IDENTITY}]{} ent2$

When an entity undergoes multiple transformations in many steps, all the state changes are recorded as a sequence of transformations that are completely anchored on textual mentions (verbs).

However, the original annotation scheme fails to address complex temporal ordering of events and temporally conditioned event dependencies. This means that the original annotation scheme cannot take into account the fact that events can happen in a different order than they are written in the source text. Therefore, annotation is done under the assumption that all events are already temporally ordered in the text, and all source texts with complex event orders are deliberately excluded from annotation.

Since all transformation processes will take time to accomplish their goal status, we argue that temporality is an important factor to consider to understand object state changes. Furthermore, we see that some temporal relations between events are working as conditional dependencies between the events. Therefore, it is even more important to precisely model the temporal and conditional relations between events. To address this problem, we implement an annotation workflow to handle a simplified interval-based temporal logic as conditional dependencies for initiation and termination of events. This example shows how the text order and the temporal order of events can differ.

(2) a. **[Shred]**$_{evt}$ the cabbage fine.
b. **[Cook]**$_{evt}$ in butter **[melted]**$_{evt}$ over low heat until **[limp]**$_{evt}$.

- text order: *shred* → *cook* → *melt* → *(be) limp*
- temporal order:
  - (*shred*, `before`, *cook*)
  - (*shred*, `independent`, *melt*)
  - (*cook*, `begun_by`, *melt*)
  - (*cook*, `ended_by`, *(be) limp*)

3.2 Sub-types of Coreference

We proposed four sub-types of coreference-under-identity in the previous work: identity, meronymy, metonymy, and change of location. However, a widely adopted set of coreference relation subtypes does not exist. Nevertheless, there is some level of consensus in near-identity studies that the degree of sameness/difference can be measured. Based on our findings, the new version of the environment is customizable with any identity-based

[1] `https://github.com/brandeis-llc/dp-cutl`

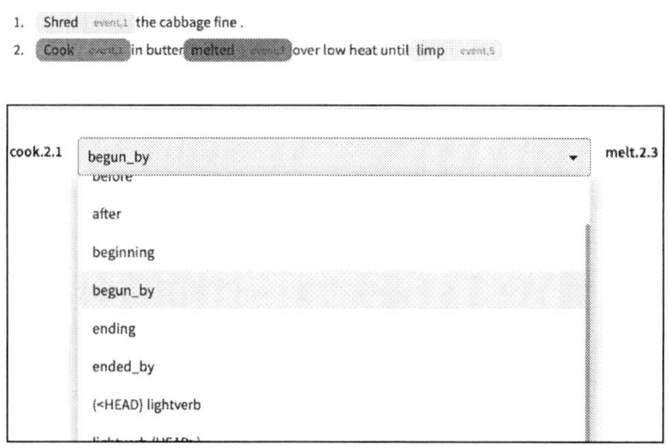

Figure 2: Event relation annotation step in CUTLER.

coreference sub-types, instead of hard-coding the relations labels into the annotation environment. New implementation enables annotation task designers to add new sub-types of coreference relations while keeping partial or total order between those relations. This flexibility allows the annotation environment to be adapted to different research needs.

4 Annotation Workflow

In this section, we overview the annotation workflow using the proposed annotation environment.

4.1 Input data

The annotation process begins with loading the input data into the environment. The environment does not support span-based mention annotation, so the input data must be pre-annotated with spans for entity and event mentions. This can be done manually or with existing NLP applications. Once the input data is pre-annotated, it can be loaded into the environment and the annotation process can begin.

4.2 Event relation annotation

First step in the annotation is to reorder event mentions based on their temporal order. From the pre-annotated list of event mentions, annotators are shown a pair of events and their surrounding text, and asked to label pairwise relation by selecting a label among

- `independent`: no temporal relation between the event pair
- `before/after`: one event must be finished before the other starts
- `beginning/begun_by`: the beginning of one event is conditioned on the end of the other (e.g., *do X immediately after Y*)
- `ending/ended_by`: the end of one event is conditioned on the end of the other (e.g., *do X until Y*)
- `light-verb-construction (LVC)`[2]: not a temporal relation, but a lexical pattern that has two separate text parts

These temporal relation names (except for `LVC`, since `LVC` is not a temporal one) are selected from TimeML's `TLINK`, but the logic is largely based on Allen, 1983. Each pairwise annotation is then used in a simplified temporal reasoning algebra to generate next prompt in real-time[3].

4.3 Coreference link annotation

For this step, we directly adopt the previous CUTLER environment. Unlike other coreference annotation tools that require annotators to link entity mentions across the whole document, CUTLER decomposes the task to individual event-level and simplifies the complex conference task into an event-argument linking task. This means that annotators only need to link entity mentions that are part of the *current* event, which is much easier than linking mentions that are spread out across a document. We add improvements

[2]for `LVC` (e.g., *[Bring]$_{evt}$ to a [boil]$_{evt}$*), annotators are asked to pick the *head* event span.

[3]the algebra is only designed to reduce the number of pairwise prompts to annotators based on transitive reduction, and thus does not aim to construct a total order of events nor a full closure of temporal relations.

1. to event argument candidate selection algorithm to handle temporally conditioned overlapping events: previously there were no overlapping events, but in the new scheme, we have end temporal relations that indicate event overlaps.

2. to the real-time graph visualization feature, based on our addition of a temporal ordering annotation step to reflect the additional time dimension: fig 1 shows examples of `independent` and `ending` relations.

4.4 Coreference sub-type annotation

Although we proposed four sub-types of identity-based coreference previously, CUTLER only implements an explicit interface for annotating meronymy relations. Other sub-types are automatically inferred by some *magic* features of the tool, based on the entity types and event argument structures. We decided to re-do the coreference labeling interface to make the environment more flexible to different definitions of coreference types, as we found different label sets from different previous work. As a result, our environment asks annotators to explicitly pick a label when a coreference link is drawn, while keeping the original magic inference feature to provide some reasonable default values to annotators.

4.5 Output data

Annotation results are stored in relation triples, readily available for graph visualization for human readers or algorithmic ingestion for machine consumption.

5 Future work

At the moment, the environment is implemented as a locally hosted web application. However, we believe that our simplified annotation scheme and annotation workflow implementation will enable a quick adoption of the environment into crowdsource annotation tool running on platforms like AMT.

6 Conclusion

In this paper, we present an integrated annotation environment that supports different aspects of event semantics and coreference relations, including full- and near-identity sub-type labeling. The environment provides simplicity for annotators for quick and easy task completion, while provides flexibility for task designers who might need to adopt different typology and definitions of coreference relations for their research needs and interests. The scheme and environment (and related code) is publicly available as an open-source software. And our future direction is to port the theoretical concepts and tool interface to a more crowdsource-friendly implementation, to continue our effort to create an event-driven coreference annotation dataset.

Limitations

This work showcases our latest tool development efforts. The environment and annotation scheme we present in this work are highly tailored for modeling conferences and event semantics in procedural text, where the majority of events are transformational (that cause a changes in states of actual objects), rather than pragmatic or speculative, and the majority of entities have denotations to real-world objects. We are also developing a set of datasets that can be used to describe the semantics of these events and entities based on the environment and scheme described in this work. However, those dataset creation efforts are beyond the scope of this paper.

Ethics Statement

This work is based on our own previous work. The previous work included human annotation effort on publicly available dataset. The source data that we used in the annotation was collections of multicultural recipes text, written in English, distributed under Creative Common license. Given the data domain, annotation methodology, and tool development, we do not anticipate any major ethical concern.

Acknowledgements

We appreciate all the valuable feedback from the anonymous reviewers. This work was supported by NSF Award #2326985.

References

James F. Allen. 1983. Maintaining knowledge about temporal intervals. *Commun. ACM*, 26(11):832–843.

Rahul Aralikatte and Anders Søgaard. 2020. Model based annotation of coreference. In *Proceedings of the Twelfth Language Resources and Evaluation Conference*, pages 74–79, Marseille, France. European Language Resources Association.

Jon Chamberlain, Massimo Poesio, and Udo Kruschwitz. 2016. Phrase detectives corpus 1.0 crowdsourced anaphoric coreference. In *Proceedings of the Tenth International Conference on Language Resources and Evaluation (LREC'16)*, pages 2039–2046, Portorož, Slovenia. European Language Resources Association (ELRA).

Bhavana Dalvi, Lifu Huang, Niket Tandon, Wen-tau Yih, and Peter Clark. 2018. Tracking state changes in procedural text: a challenge dataset and models for process paragraph comprehension. In *Proceedings of the 2018 Conference of the North American Chapter of the Association for Computational Linguistics: Human Language Technologies, Volume 1 (Long Papers)*, pages 1595–1604, New Orleans, Louisiana. Association for Computational Linguistics.

George Doddington, Alexis Mitchell, Mark Przybocki, Lance Ramshaw, Stephanie Strassel, and Ralph Weischedel. 2004. The automatic content extraction (ACE) program – tasks, data, and evaluation. In *Proceedings of the Fourth International Conference on Language Resources and Evaluation (LREC'04)*, Lisbon, Portugal. European Language Resources Association (ELRA).

Biaoyan Fang, Timothy Baldwin, and Karin Verspoor. 2022. What does it take to bake a cake? the RecipeRef corpus and anaphora resolution in procedural text. In *Findings of the Association for Computational Linguistics: ACL 2022*, pages 3481–3495, Dublin, Ireland. Association for Computational Linguistics.

Ralph Grishman and Beth Sundheim. 1996. Message Understanding Conference- 6: A brief history. In *COLING 1996 Volume 1: The 16th International Conference on Computational Linguistics*.

Ankita Gupta, Marzena Karpinska, Wenlong Zhao, Kalpesh Krishna, Jack Merullo, Luke Yeh, Mohit Iyyer, and Brendan O'Connor. 2023. ezCoref: Towards unifying annotation guidelines for coreference resolution. In *Findings of the Association for Computational Linguistics: EACL 2023*, pages 312–330, Dubrovnik, Croatia. Association for Computational Linguistics.

Lynette Hirschman and Nancy Chinchor. 1998. Appendix F: MUC-7 coreference task definition (version 3.0). In *Seventh Message Understanding Conference (MUC-7): Proceedings of a Conference Held in Fairfax, Virginia, April 29 - May 1, 1998*.

Eduard Hovy, Mitchell Marcus, Martha Palmer, Lance Ramshaw, and Ralph Weischedel. 2006. OntoNotes: The 90% solution. In *Proceedings of the Human Language Technology Conference of the NAACL, Companion Volume: Short Papers*, pages 57–60, New York City, USA. Association for Computational Linguistics.

Shinsuke Mori, Hirokuni Maeta, Yoko Yamakata, and Tetsuro Sasada. 2014. Flow graph corpus from recipe texts. In *Proceedings of the Ninth International Conference on Language Resources and Evaluation (LREC'14)*, pages 2370–2377, Reykjavik, Iceland. European Language Resources Association (ELRA).

Christoph Müller and Michael Strube. 2006. Multi-level annotation of linguistic data with MMAX2. In Sabine Braun, Kurt Kohn, and Joybrato Mukherjee, editors, *Corpus Technology and Language Pedagogy: New Resources, New Tools, New Methods*, pages 197–214. Peter Lang, Frankfurt a.M., Germany.

Bruno Oberle. 2018. SACR: A drag-and-drop based tool for coreference annotation. In *Proceedings of the Eleventh International Conference on Language Resources and Evaluation (LREC 2018)*, Miyazaki, Japan. European Language Resources Association (ELRA).

Massimo Poesio and Ron Artstein. 2008. Anaphoric Annotation in the ARRAU Corpus. In *Proceedings of the Sixth International Conference on Language Resources and Evaluation (LREC'08)*, Marrakech, Morocco. European Language Resources Association (ELRA).

Massimo Poesio, Patrick Sturt, Ron Artstein, and Ruth Filik. 2006. Underspecification and Anaphora: Theoretical Issues and Preliminary Evidence. *Discourse Processes*, 42(2):157–175.

Sameer Pradhan, Alessandro Moschitti, Nianwen Xue, Olga Uryupina, and Yuchen Zhang. 2012. CoNLL-2012 shared task: Modeling multilingual unrestricted coreference in OntoNotes. In *Joint Conference on EMNLP and CoNLL - Shared Task*, pages 1–40, Jeju Island, Korea. Association for Computational Linguistics.

Sameer Pradhan, Lance Ramshaw, Mitchell Marcus, Martha Palmer, Ralph Weischedel, and Nianwen Xue. 2011. CoNLL-2011 shared task: Modeling unrestricted coreference in OntoNotes. In *Proceedings of the Fifteenth Conference on Computational Natural Language Learning: Shared Task*, pages 1–27, Portland, Oregon, USA. Association for Computational Linguistics.

Jakob Prange, Nathan Schneider, and Omri Abend. 2019. Semantically constrained multilayer annotation: The case of coreference. In *Proceedings of the First International Workshop on Designing Meaning Representations*, pages 164–176, Florence, Italy. Association for Computational Linguistics.

Marta Recasens, Eduard Hovy, and M Antonia Martı. 2010. A Typology of Near-Identity Relations for Coreference (NIDENT). In *LREC2010*.

Nils Reiter. 2018. CorefAnnotator - A New Annotation Tool for Entity References. In *Abstracts of EADH: Data in the Digital Humanities*.

Kyeongmin Rim, Jingxuan Tu, Bingyang Ye, Marc Verhagen, Eben Holderness, and James Pustejovsky.

2023. The Coreference under Transformation Labeling Dataset: Entity Tracking in Procedural Texts Using Event Models. In *Findings of the Association for Computational Linguistics: ACL 2023*, pages 12448–12460, Toronto, Canada. Association for Computational Linguistics.

Ina Roesiger, Arndt Riester, and Jonas Kuhn. 2018. Bridging resolution: Task definition, corpus resources and rule-based experiments. In *Proceedings of the 27th International Conference on Computational Linguistics*, pages 3516–3528, Santa Fe, New Mexico, USA. Association for Computational Linguistics.

Niket Tandon, Keisuke Sakaguchi, Bhavana Dalvi, Dheeraj Rajagopal, Peter Clark, Michal Guerquin, Kyle Richardson, and Eduard Hovy. 2020. A Dataset for Tracking Entities in Open Domain Procedural Text. In *Proceedings of the 2020 Conference on Empirical Methods in Natural Language Processing (EMNLP)*, pages 6408–6417, Online. Association for Computational Linguistics.

Olga Uryupina, Ron Artstein, Antonella Bristot, Federica Cavicchio, Kepa Rodriguez, and Massimo Poesio. 2016. ARRAU: Linguistically-motivated annotation of anaphoric descriptions. In *Proceedings of the Tenth International Conference on Language Resources and Evaluation (LREC'16)*, pages 2058–2062, Portorož, Slovenia. European Language Resources Association (ELRA).

Antoine Widlöcher and Yann Mathet. 2012. The glozz platform: A corpus annotation and mining tool. In *Proceedings of the 2012 ACM Symposium on Document Engineering*, DocEng '12, page 171–180, New York, NY, USA. Association for Computing Machinery.

Xueqing Wu, Sha Li, and Heng Ji. 2023. OpenPI-C: A better benchmark and stronger baseline for open-vocabulary state tracking. In *Findings of the Association for Computational Linguistics: ACL 2023*, pages 7213–7222, Toronto, Canada. Association for Computational Linguistics.

Amir Zeldes. 2022. Opinion Piece: Can we Fix the Scope for Coreference?: Problems and Solutions for Benchmarks beyond OntoNotes. *Dialogue & Discourse*, 13(1):41–62.

Author Index

Association for Computational Linguistics
209 N. Eighth Street
Stroudsburg, Pennsylvania 18360

ISBN 978-1-7138-8598-6

CURRAN ASSOCIATES INC.
proceedings
.com